Entertainment 101

Entertainment 101

an industry primer

101

rodger w. claire

CONTRIBUTING WRITERS

john d. boswell

julie dufine

helene goldsen

jeffrey hirsch

steve root

amanda rudolph

sandy wells

POMEGRANATE PRESS LTD.

BEVERLY HILLS   LONDON

acknowledgments

We gratefully acknowledge the generosity and expert
advice of Steven A. Bell, Jonathan Black, John D. Boswell,
Rodger Brown, Jay Cooper, Gordon Davidson, Susan Deetz,
E! Online, Bill Farley, Frazier Mountain Internet,
Lew Harris, Robert Masselo, Stephen Randall, Jeff Rose,
Joan Stein, Mary Jane Ufland and Lawrence Turman.

Keep updated with the E101 Network Web site: www.E101.net

The digital revolution is radically changing the creative, business, legal and
technology landscape of the entertainment industry. Keep that competitive
edge and make new industry contacts at:

 **www.E101.net.**

This is a Pomegranate Press, Ltd. book.

Entertainment 101: An Industry Primer

Library of Congress Catalog Card Number: 99-63659

Softcover ISBN: 0-938817-16-7

First Printing 1999

2 4 6 8 10 9 7 5 3 1

Cover and Interior Design: *Cheryl Carrington*

Printed and bound in the United States of America

POMEGRANATE PRESS, LTD.
P.O. Box 17217
Beverly Hills, CA 90209
fax: 310•271•4930
http://www.pompress.com

contents

As more technology, toys and even new media
come to the stage, what is the direction theater
will take in the next decade?

Radio   181

Hollywood never really was, and yet it will ever be. Even in its earliest incarnation, the entertainment industry in Southern California stretched well beyond the physical environs of the "Hollywoodland" development to the desert, to the sea, to the then-lush San Fernando Valley and beyond. But the heart—some might say the brain—

of the industry has remained in the city with the world-famous zip code, Beverly Hills, even though the physical production (of motion pictures, then television series, then home videos, music CDs, new media) has spread throughout the region.

Why Beverly Hills? Because within the 5.6 square miles of this globally renowned municipality live and work so many of the movers and shakers—the dealmakers—who make the Hollywood dream factory a reality.

Only 33,000 people actually live in Beverly Hills, but each workday more than 200,000 people cross our borders. They are the agents, managers, attorneys, production executives, music moguls and behind-the-scenes support providers who fuel the engine of Hollywood's creativity. They are the doctors, dentists, restaurateurs and retailers who serve the entertainment industry's ever-growing needs.

When I was elected president of the Beverly Hills Chamber of Commerce, I looked for a tangible footprint of this massive entertainment community. To my astonishment, I found none. There was no single source that detailed how "Hollywood" works and documented the tasks and the contributions of so many of our residents and industry workers.

Even more surprising to me, no publication existed in Beverly Hills or elsewhere which could serve as a primer for "civilians" wishing to enter the entertainment business or simply to understand what it is all about.

To that end, through the underwriting of Playboy Enterprises, Inc. and Pomegranate Press, Inc.—both with offices in Beverly Hills—the Beverly Hills Chamber of

Commerce has created this unique guide to the basics, the fundamentals, of the entertainment industry.

Because this unique business often thrives on rapid change, regular updates will be forthcoming. For now, you will find core information about the business unavailable anywhere else here in Volume One, Number One.

— Richard Rosenzweig

irving berlin had it right

There really is no business like show business—never more true than on the eve of the 21st century. The last true American industry, "Hollywood" stretches from Manhattan to Silicon Valley, a huge, multibillion-dollar-a-year business that dominates the world marketplace, indeed the global culture, virtually unchallenged in its creative, technological, marketing and artistic know-how.

The tiniest nation can design a car—and can, and does—make movies. Most of our steel is imported these days. Texas' plains contain tiny pools compared to Middle Eastern deserts floating on seas of oil. But no one challenges Hollywood's hegemony in entertainment media. Our films today earn more in foreign sales than domestic take, our TV programs are seen by hundreds of millions around the globe, our pop music is the international gold standard, our Web sites and new media at the heart of the Computer Age are technological toddlers which will soon grow and redefine the very notion of entertainment in the next millennium.

Straddling the end of its first 100 years and the dawn of its next 1,000, the entertainment industry is growing so rapidly even those in the business are scrambling to keep pace. It is bigger, more complex and more robust than at anytime in its history. It is a great moment for those in the business, and an especially propitious one for those on the docks ready to embark on what may be American industry's most exciting journey yet.

Let's Take a Meeting

The bromide "It's not *what* you know, it's *who* you know" is a truism in any business—in Hollywood, it's an immutable law. There are as many ways of breaking into the business as there are individuals with imagination determined to get themselves in. A well-told tale recounts how

Steven Spielberg, a young film-crazed kid from California State University, Long Beach, jumped the back fence of Universal Studios and set up shop as a producer in an empty bungalow on the Universal back lot. Some roads in, however, are more well traveled than others. All, however, end in the same place—someone's office. In order to get a project developed, would-be filmmakers have to know who the players are and what they do. That is not an easy task in a business in which not only a person's title, but his or her order of appearance and even the type size on a video or CD jacket is wrangled over by high-priced attorneys. A single movie or television production, for example, will list a gaggle of producers—"executive producers," "associate producers," "co-producers," "line producers." But only one of those producers is the guy who really runs the show.

Entertainment 101 is a guide to this mythical, mystical, confusing world of entertainment—and the people who rule it and run it. To simplify things, we have divided the far-flung and variegated entertainment industry into its six principle businesses. film, television, music, new media, theater and radio.

To help understand how a project is actually created and to identify the players in each medium, we have listed the typical cast and crew credits from a film, a television show, a record album, a stage play, an online magazine and a radio show. We have described in detail the jobs of each artist and artisan and what they contribute to the artwork.

A project's credits, however delicately composed (and negotiated!), do not reflect the most basic—and important— truth about the pecking order in the entertainment industry:

the Great Divide between "above the line" and "below the line" players. These terms are taken from the standard motion picture budget, which actually lists producers, directors, actors and writers *above* a line on the budget sheet and everyone else *below*. Over the years, the terms have come to define the distinction between the so-called "creative" cast (star, writer, director, producer) and the artisans and craftspeople (electricians, cameramen, best boys and others) who toil on and off the set to transform a script into a movie.

It is the above-the-line members of the entertainment community who have the creativity and marketability, and thus the clout, to nurture and develop a project, attach talent to it, then bring it to a studio or independent film company, network, theater, record label or online service provider to clasp the Holy Grail of all entertainment players: financing. Though the terms are customarily applied only to the film business, for purposes of this book, they will distinguish the difference between the creative talent controlling a project (by contract) and the all-important craftspeople and artisans who transform an initial idea into a finished vision—a tangible work of art or commerce.

Entertainment 101 is designed to offer a broad, knowledgeable overview of the entire entertainment industry as it exists at the portal of the next millennium. It defines the many artists whose craftsmanship creates the beauty of the final work. It offers an incisive look at the rules and realities that govern each of the industry's six major businesses, the challenges, promises and possibilities as they exist at the end of the 20th century and the beginning of the 21st.

For the mogul-minded, the curious, or even a business-person looking to break into a new marketplace, this book is a blueprint of how to break into a seemingly closed society. *Entertainment 101* is a guide into the inner workings of this culture, deciphering its rules, its language, its codes and its finely nuanced, ever-changing pecking order. ∎

film

Hollywood, of course, is an idea, not a place; a concept, not a zip code. That's not to say there is no community called "Hollywood." In fact, Los Angeles County has two: the city of West Hollywood, an incorporated city next door to Beverly Hills; and Hollywood, a part of the city of Los

Angeles, lying roughly between West Hollywood and downtown Los Angeles. It was always, it seems, set up to be a little more than it really was, originally dubbed "Hollywoodland" back in the 1920s by a developer with an outsized love of holly bushes and a nose for marketing. Today, it is a mostly declining district of fast-food outlets, ethnic eateries and tourist shops targeted for urban renewal and dotted by an occasional landmark from better days gone by, like the Chinese or Egyptian theaters. The grandest thing about it is its name. But even in that Golden Age, Hollywood was never the epicenter of the motion picture industry, despite its boulevard sidewalks lined with the famed "Walk of Stars." The closest studio is Paramount, its famed studio gates fronting Melrose Avenue in a decayed no-man's-land miles from Hollywood Boulevard. Even then, the stars lived in Beverly Hills or west, up the coast in Malibu.

What has been called "Hollywood" for most of its history is really the collection of motion picture studios founded across Los Angeles County, from Culver City to Burbank, in the early part of the 20th century by such tough-minded, ironfisted moguls as Adolph Zukor, Louis B. Mayer, Samuel Goldwyn, Jack L. Warner, William Fox, Carl Laemmle and others who came west with a vision of making motion pictures for the masses—not to mention a fast buck or two. The results were the first seven studios, affectionately to be known as the "Seven Sisters": Twentieth Century Fox, Metro-Goldwyn-Mayer, Columbia Pictures, Paramount, Universal, United Artists and Warner Bros.

For decades, the so-called "studio system" functioned more or less as a monopoly, each studio signing actors, directors and writers to long-term contracts which bound them exclusively to the particular studio. Through this profitable but semi-indentured employment, the moguls controlled every facet of their business, from careers to the kinds of movies that were produced. If a star or director wanted to make a project for another studio, he had to get permission from his own studio, which routinely demanded lucrative quid pro quos. (A clue to how the early moguls saw themselves can be gleaned by the interior design choices of much-hated Columbia chieftain Harry Cohn, whose all-white office and ship-deck-sized desk were conceived to the smallest detail to replicate Benito Mussolini's.)

These days, of course, the industry is as competitive as the aluminum-siding business—and about as friendly. The studios' monopoly of the business began to crack with the famous consent decree that took theater ownership away from the studios. Meanwhile, a new breed of tough, bare-knuckle agents led by Myron Selznick finally broke the back of the studio system. Nowadays, Hollywood's once-hated caste structure is but a historical footnote, a concept as familiar to today's teen-movie heartthrobs as the "behavior clause" (a contract rider governing a star's moral comportment off the set that no self-respecting executive would have left the bargaining table without). The moguls had all worked together to preserve their power, though they often couldn't stand the sight of one another. By contrast, the studios today are owned by "faceless" global entertainment conglomerates (though that does not preclude the occasional personal skirmish between competing egos. Witness the animus between

News Corporation's Rupert Murdoch and Time Warner's Ted Turner or Disney's Michael Eisner and DreamWorks' Jeffrey Katzenberg.

Some studios have changed corporate hands numerous times since the founding moguls, like mountain climbers clinging to a safety rope, let go one by one, surrendering their beloved studios to a new generation of bottom-line corporate accountants and attorneys. Columbia is owned by Japanese electronics giant Sony; Universal by Canadian distiller Seagram; Paramount by cable behemoth Viacom; Twentieth Century Fox by Rupert Murdoch's News Corporation; MGM (as of this writing) by financier Kirk Kerkorian; Warner Bros. by Time Warner; United Artists, the onetime "artists" studio founded by Charlie Chaplin, by Mary Pickford and Douglas Fairbanks, a poor stepsister to Kerkorian's MGM. Most no longer are merely motion picture studios but global entertainment empires, with huge presences in television, recording, new media and Internet destinations, video, theater, theme parks and even newspapers and magazines.

In addition, the Seven Sisters are no longer alone in the marketplace. Sony, for instance, also began TriStar in the 1980s to extend Columbia's penetration of the marketplace, though its feature-film division has been disbanded in recent years. The Walt Disney Company has become one of Hollywood's "G-8," as it were, with global interests in every facet of the entertainment business, including its ownership of Miramax. And there is DreamWorks SKG, a company in search of a studio, which was founded by record mogul David Geffen, director Steven Spielberg and ex-Disney chief Jeffrey Katzenberg. Independent production companies also play a huge role nowadays. Run by successful producers or former studio executives and backed by their own financing, independents function much the same as the studios, though they lack the distribution and, in most cases, the marketing resources of the majors. A "small-movie" company like Miramax, for instance, operates virtually autonomously, but its ownership by Disney gives it a major's clout, allowing it to compete for bigger projects and bigger stars.

But what exactly does a studio do?

In simple terms, studios finance and distribute movies to the theaters. They put together all the elements of a film, acquiring the script or original source material, developing the story and screenplay, hiring the director, casting the movie and so on. The studio also finances the project, paying the salaries (or splitting the profits with the major talent), paying the insurance, the overhead, servicing the debt, etc. The major studios provide the equipment, including the cameras, tracks, booms, hundreds of miles of electrical cable, dollies, etc., the back lot for shoots, transportation for location shoots, and lodging, food (in the form of per diems or catered on the set) and star trailers. The studio also markets and distributes the film, both domestically and abroad. The studio almost always owns the negative, which becomes part of its library. It makes its income in collecting the rental fees for domestic and, in most cases, foreign releases, for television broadcasting worldwide, for video, laser and DVD release, for theatrical rereleases and for any projects which grow out of the film, including sequels, plays, books, remakes and the like.

This simple formula is, naturally, infinitely more complex in practice. For one thing, expensive action-adventure films with huge special effects budgets are more and more often being co-produced with rival studios. Many films are co-produced by independent companies, which lack distribution and cash and must go to major studios, striking complicated profit-sharing agreements, dividing up slices of the domestic, foreign and video pie in myriad ways.

The rise of star-power agents and agencies in the 1980s, too, has inexorably changed the business of Hollywood. Increasingly in the 1980s, corporate owners based in New York or Japan demanded routine profit predictions and bottom-line performance from their studio subsidiaries much the same way they would, say, their VCR or video-rental businesses. They wanted to know what the product line was for any given quarter, how much it was going to cost to produce and, to the nearest dollar, what the predicted sales—and profit—would be.

But the motion picture business is not like the usual corporate business. Its product is a creative work. No one can possibly know how an audience, millions and millions of diverse people, is going to react to something make-believe. Each film, in truth, is a crapshoot. A studio president can try to minimize his or her losses by greenlighting (putting into production) a certain kind of film or film genre which has performed well in the past. For further insurance, the studio then looks to attach a proven director and an actor with a proven box-office track record. But, unhappily, time and again, that formula has not guaranteed success. Often, the results are disastrous. Nonetheless, the corporate owners, who usually understand little of the subtleties of the film business, continue to demand sure things from their beleaguered executives. The studio chieftains—sometimes recently arrived heads replacing heads already rolled and whose own slate of movies take one to two years to move from concept to completion—are under the gun to produce hits fast.

In the late 1970s, studio heads began turning to agents for help. Agents controlled the writers, directors and actors the studios needed to make movies. The big agencies controlled the big-name writers, directors and actors the studio presidents perceived as a form of insurance for their films. Knowing that a studio president who wanted a particular client was under the gun—and that his counterpart across town was under a similar corporate gun and just as eager for the agent's client—allowed the agency to squeeze more concessions out of the studio. So-called "packaging" was one of these major concessions. An integral part of the television business, packaging became routine in motion picture deal-making. The old-time moguls and executives prided themselves on their casting of pictures. But by the 1980s, an agency which controlled a writer who had a hot script would routinely also attach a director, one or two major stars and maybe even a producer, then offer the entire "package" to a studio to bid on. Many studio executives, like Joe Roth at Twentieth Century Fox and Jeffrey Katzenberg at Disney, bristled at high-priced packaging, which not only drove up the cost of a film but also allowed an agent to take over a creative function of the studio. But if a studio head balked at a package, the agent simply moved on to a competitor who was more desperate and had fewer qualms about paying the price. The result was such

'80s high-priced disappointments as CAA's Robert Redford-Debra Winger package, *Legal Eagles,* and the Sean Connery-Dustin Hoffman picture *Family Business.*

This practice shifted power from the studios to the agencies and the stars. To stay competitive, studio heads tried to ally themselves with powerful producers, directors and actors, offering not only unheard-of salaries of up to $20 million a picture for a few top stars, but also lucrative housekeeping and first-look deals which literally brought the producers and talent onto the studio lot.

Warner Bros.' famed, long-running team of Robert Daley and Terry Semel was the pairing of two quintessential studio dons of the '80s. Mentored by Warner's celebrated chief, Steve Ross, famous for his lavish courting of stars and talent, Daley and Semel continued the tradition of company jets, lavish gifts and the infamous Acapulco villa with its Olympic-size pool, which was loaned out to stars and executives as a bonus for being part of the Warner "family." The two chieftains courted stars and directors with charm and perks, making Warner the studio where filmmakers wanted to be. The other studios, too, offered sweetened deals to keep their stars in the stable. By the end of the '80s, there was hardly a bankable star who didn't have his or her own production company.

Whenever a major star left a studio, there was a scramble by rival studios to land him or her. Perks usually included a first-look deal for the star's production company, in which the studio was obligated to at least consider, and usually develop a certain number of projects that were put into the pipeline by the actor's company. Other housekeeping deals stipulated that the studio provide office space for the production company, pay for the company's development people and even, at times, include such perks as fuel and a flight crew for the star's personal jet, a masseuse and, not unheard of, a condo every now and then. (Years back, it was reported that Paramount, in order to land Tom Cruise, agreed to use on all his films a new state-of-the-art sound machine developed by a fellow member of the actor's Church of Scientology.)

In Hollywood, everything old is new again. By the latter half of the 1990s, the balance of power began tipping back to the studio side of the scales, as studios, finding themselves reduced to midsized operating units of huge entertainment concerns, were pressured by their corporate bosses to deal with the new math; rising costs that were far outstripping single-digit returns on investment.

If their '80s counterparts offered up pricey star packages in an effort to somehow guarantee success in the "voodoo" of box-office economics, late-'90s studio chieftains began returning to the much more time-honored practice of risk-cutting: slashing costs. Indeed, the studios had little choice. The average cost of making a film doubled between 1993 and 1998, from $26.1 million to $52.7 million. Marketing costs shot up 79 percent. Likewise, film and entertainment revenues began to account for less of a corporation's bottom line. In 1988, films and TV produced 68 percent of revenues at Paramount Communications; a decade later they had dropped to 39 percent of Viacom sales. At Time Warner, they dropped from 37 percent to roughly 30 percent.

Worse, the growth rate in worldwide revenue dropped from 15 percent a year to below 5 percent in 1998. Total box-office receipts accounted for less and less of film revenue, dropping from 35 percent in 1990 to 24 percent in 1998. It soon became clear to the corporate owners that the real value of film lay not so much in huge immediate box-office returns, but as product to feed their cable and television units, while adding to the ultimate worth of a studio—its film library.

Meanwhile, studio heads suffered the "New Line factor," a production entity acquired in Time Warner's merger with Ted Turner's entertainment empire. While big-studio rivals suffered through box-office disappointments like *Wild Wild West,* New Line boasted glowing earning reports, cranking out hip, low-budget teen fare like *Austin Powers: The Spy Who Shagged Me* for half the price of the usual big-ticket Hollywood film. In addition, small movies like *The Blair Witch Project*, passed on by most of the majors and made for the price of a student film, raked in tens of millions of dollars for tiny Artisan Entertainment.

Corporate Hollywood paranoia was nothing new, though much of the business press seemed to greet Hollywood's late-'90s retrenchment as something akin to a financial tribulation. In the early '80s, as a number of studios continued to suffer financial setbacks following their corporate mergers in the '70s, many new owners turned to attorneys and financial executives to pull in the fiscal reins. Financier Kirk Kerkorian appointed his former attorney and CEO Frank Rothman, to helm MGM in 1981 and newly merged MGM/UA in 1983. Investment banker Herbert Allen brought in longtime investment banker friend Alan Hirschfeld in 1981 to stop the bleeding at Columbia Pictures. Five years later, when he laid the company off to Coca-Cola for $750 million Alan appointed ex-Securities and Exchange executive Charles Francis T. "Fay" Vincent to oversee the company for the soft drink giant. When Columbia started sister studio TriStar, entertainment attorney Gary Handler was hired to help run the feature division. In 1986 Universal hired another well-known entertainment attorney, Tom Pollock, to clean up shop.

Once again at the end of the '90s, corporate owners began turning to attorneys and financial strongmen to keep watch over their studio bottom lines. After Daley and Semel stunned Hollywood by resigning as Warner co-chairmen in July 1999, Time Warner replaced the last of the old-style Hollywood heads with a former attorney, Barry Meyer. Likewise, Universal Pictures appointed onetime CPA Brian Mulligan as co-chairman of Universal Pictures and MGM tapped Chris McGurk, a former financial executive at Pepsi, to turn around its floundering studio. Indeed, Paramount requires Chairwoman Sherry Lansing to receive the blessing of Viacom Entertainment chairman Jonathan Dolgen before she can greenlight a movie.

The first thing studios did was cut back the number of films they would make a year. Though huge stars and directors still command large salaries to open a picture, studios were not so keen about greenlighting projects they considered risky, blithely dumping big-name stars (and their $15 million salaries) and even writer-directors from projects with an abandon that would have produced flop sweats in any studio executive just 10 years ago. Studio heads also began ordering producers to cut budgets as much as 30 percent. If they couldn't cut out enough, then stars were dropped.

Faced with less work and fewer movies, actors and directors, especially those considered mid-range, have quietly

Ironically, the man who revolutionized the accounting practices of Hollywood was the soft-spoken, self-effacing James Stewart. In 1950, Universal was developing the studio's first big Western in years, *Winchester '73*. It had already cast its own $75-a-week contract players Rock Hudson and Shelley Winters. The financially troubled studio badly wanted Stewart, the quintessential American cowboy. Legendary agent Lew Wasserman knew Universal was desperate for a hit—and would pay almost anything to get Stewart. At the time, Hollywood's biggest star, Clark Gable, was getting $300,000 per picture.

But in Stewart's case, Wasserman refused a flat salary and instead demanded a percentage of the film's net profits. Universal reluctantly agreed. The deal made Stewart a then-staggering $600,000. More importantly, however, Wasserman created the two words which would signal the death of the old-time studio system: back end.

Profit participation would quickly redefine deal making in Hollywood. For starters, there was net profit and gross profit. Net profit was a percentage of actual profits after the studio deducted the cost of making the picture, creating the prints and distributing the movie. Eventually, studio accountants found there were many deductions to make before net profit could be divvied up—distribution, marketing, sales and advertising costs, not to mention overhead and depreciation.

Not to be outflanked, agents began taking aim at the film's gross profit. But with second releases, foreign releases and, later, television and videocassette sales, gross profit was hard to compute. Some stars began taking back-end money up front based on an agreed-upon calculation of what the film would make. The problem with this formula was that it meant both the stars and the studios had to read the future.

Eventually, three versions of gross participation emerged. Rolling gross and adjusted gross acknowledged the legitimacy of certain expenses which studios incurred in producing and distributing a film. An A-list star, the only kind who's going to rate gross instead of net in the first place, starts receiving back-end money after a certain agreed upon figure is reached. Under rolling gross, expenses include the "negative cost" of the film—what it actually costs to shoot the movie. They also cover the studio's overhead, that is, everything from the producer's office space to staff salaries to insurance premiums and even the interest on the overhead. Rolling gross takes into account any back-end participation given to the film's director and actor(s). Adjusted gross is essentially another version of rolling gross, but includes even more negative costs such as advertising and marketing expenditures.

Even so, adjusted gross is often perceived to be better than rolling gross because it kicks in the first time an agreed-upon recoupment level is achieved. After that, many costs cease to be included. The Holy Grail of back-end deal making, however, is a third option, known as true gross or first dollar gross. This is what AAA stars and directors receive: a percentage of profits from the sale of the first ticket. Thus the mystery is solved as to how even Kim Basinger could afford to buy her very own Georgia town. ▶

taken large pay cuts to do projects. Similarly, unknowns and young talent are getting more shots at jobs that would once have gone to high-priced established talent. Increasingly, studios have focused more on finding small, relatively low-budget movies that they can acquire in finished form, like *The Full Monty*, the classic *Four Weddings and a Funeral* or even Oscar-winner *Life is Beautiful*, films which find a loyal crossover audience, generate long-term income and add to the prestige of a studio's library.

Such is the New Math—that is until the next blockbuster starts the next trend and Hollywood, always looking for the big hit, the big rush, sees the rise of the next new studio system.

Typically, a studio is headed by a chairman and/or CEO. Beneath are the various department and division heads: marketing, filmed entertainment, production, distribution, recording, television, theme parks and the like. Reporting directly to the chairman is the president of the film division. Many studio presidents, unlike the old moguls, are former successful producers like Disney's Joe Roth, Paramount's Sherry Lansing and Sony's John Calley. As producers, they not only know how to develop and produce a motion picture but have the relationships and deal-making knowledge to bring the best talent to the studio. Occasionally, a president is a former entertainment or corporate attorney. Hollywood had a long tradition of agents jumping to the creative end, like Charles K. Feldman and Lew Wasserman. The '70s and '80s saw many of their colleagues take the same leap as the legendary Freddie Fields and the late David Begelman, ICM's Guy McElwaine, and later CAA agents Mike Menchel and founding partner Ron Meyer.

Though it varies widely from studio to studio, the president usually has greenlight authority, the power to fund and give a movie in development the go-ahead to be filmed. The studio head is also responsible for putting together a budget and a slate of films—a mix of big-budget action pics, romantic comedies, small adult movies and so on—that the studio will release. He or she is responsible for creating the relationships with powerful producers and big-name stars that a studio needs to legitimize itself and its movies. All of this is done with input from the chairman and the studio's top executives. Disney chief Michael Eisner, for example, is known to involve himself not only in casting but marketing and distribution decisions.

Powerful producers and top stars usually pitch their projects directly to the president or even the chairman, sometimes over dinner or in a corner at an industry function. Producers who are not as powerful pitch to any number of executives or vice-presidents beneath the studio president. These executives stay current with what projects have been put into development or greenlighted by rival studios. In addition, these executives also keeps tabs on projects greenlighted under their watch, troubleshooting problems with the producer and smoothing out contractual and legal entanglements.

Writers and newly arrived movie producers with no clout and no contacts usually pitch to what are known in the industry, somewhat derogatorily, as "D-girls," development execs who have no greenlighting authority and little access to the studio head. The development executive's job, like readers at a publishing house, is to weed out ideas and scripts that are patently noncommercial. They also, however, recommend to his or her boss scripts, plays, books, magazine articles or pitches that sound promising—hoping, like their bosses, to find that one-in-a-million original project that will become the next *Lethal Weapon*.

Projects arrive at a studio through several routes. They can be pitched by an independent producer, who normally has already cut a deal with the writer and/or director, promising many things that the studio now has to deliver when it steps into the producer's shoes on a deal. A project can be purchased in "turnaround" from another studio. That happens when a studio has developed a script but decided not to got forward with the project, offering the movie up to any studio who will reimburse its costs up to that point.

Projects also can be purchased directly by the studio; for instance, a studio head purchases a project as another medium, say, in the form of the rights to a hit play or best-seller. Studios usually purchase these rights at the request of one of their producers or with a particular producer and/or director in mind. A studio head looking for, say, Sydney Pollack to direct the latest John Grisham best-seller will give the project to Pollack's production company.

The producer then hires an acceptable writer and works to develop a script, with or without the participation of the studio executive. Once he has a shootable script, a process that requires many rewrites and, more often than not, several screenwriters, the producer, working with the studio executives, casts the film's key players.

The agents, the studio executives and the producer then outline the broad deal points for all the talent. At this point, the studio's legal affairs department takes over, and the deal points are hammered out in a long, excruciating, sometimes torturous, negotiation dance, often requiring the reentry of the studio president—and even chairman—at least once to work out a compromise on the potential deal breaker that neither side will give in to.

When the script (not always finished), the director and the actors are all onboard, the studio president green-lights the movie, which goes from preproduction to principal photography, or actual shooting. By this time, the producer and director have hired the crew, scouted the locations, annotated their scripts, secured the cameras and film and are ready to roll. Shooting schedules run anywhere from six weeks to six months, though numerous projects beyond the initial scheduling due to any number of logistical and contractual problems that inevitably raise their ugly heads during the course of any production.

When the principal photography is completed, the film goes into postproduction, either at special postproduction studios scattered from Santa Monica to Burbank to Hollywood or back on the studio lot itself. Special effects work is done at a special F/X production facility like George Lucas's Industrial Light & Magic. Finally, the director hands in his "director's cut," his own vision of the movie, edited in accordance with his contract, which stipulates the rating the film must qualify for and the length, a critical concern to studios who need to placate theater owners who want to show a film as many times as possible during the day.

The film is then screened for the studio brass. The president, perhaps even the chairman through his executives, gives the producer and director notes for suggested changes in pacing, tone, cutting, etc. Heated debate—even screaming—is not uncommon, but compromises are usually made to mollify both the director and the studio. Once the movie is cut to everyone's satisfaction, the marketing and distribution people go to work on positioning the film for a propitious release date, one that will not run the film up against another summer blockbuster opening on the same summer weekend. Hundreds of prints are ordered and carefully guarded from piracy, the one-sheets (the movie posters) are printed, the publicists are put into action rounding up the press and finally, the film screens with the entire studio management holding its collective breath until the weekend returns can be counted. Then the whole process is started anew with the next hot project. ■

Names You'll Never See on a Credit Sheet . . . but Without Whom There Would Be No Deal

Talent Agent

Praised, despised. Armani-clad, stylish, cigar-chomping boor. Best friend, heartless shark. However perceived, the agent is, simply put, indispensable to the industry. He is the worker bee, pollinating and cross-pollinating a field of flowering talent, creating the relationships that drive the business of moviemaking. There are literary agents for writers, talent agents for actors, agents for directors, sometimes even agents for producers. They work individually in small boutiques or as part of huge institutions with huge resources and powerful motion picture, television, literary and theatrical departments. An agent's job is to find work for his client, to negotiate his salary and ensure his working conditions. He is protector, enforcer, hand-holder, but above all, deal maker. Agents are licensed by the state and franchised by the numerous motion picture and television guilds.

For his work, an agent by law can charge no more than 10 percent of a client's salary. Agencies, however, quickly found a more imaginative and lucrative means of charging for their services. The con-cept of packaging began in television (See "Let's Make a Deal" in "Television") and was adapted in modified form to feature-film deals. An agency typically puts together the key elements of a project—the writer, the director and the star—and then sells the entire "package" to a studio for one huge fee rather than commissioning each separate client's deal. Agency clients like the practice, because the studios end up paying their commission as a kind of surcharge. The agency likes the practice because it sometimes could charge as much as 10 percent of the project's budget. Even some studio heads like the practice because they could buy a talent-laden project all cast and ready to go. But such packages drove up the cost of making a movie, and agencies have been blamed for the astronomical rise in star salaries and for using the clout of their star actors and directors to gouge studios for huge fees.

Agents have the material, they have the stars, they have the directors, they have the relationships with producers and studios, making them among the most powerful individuals in Hollywood. In the 1980s, huge successes like Creative Artists Agency, International Creative Management, William Morris Agency and United Talent Agency became bedrock institutions of Hollywood, rivaling the power of the studios. Meanwhile, many top agents have gone on to run studios, leaving some to wonder who's agenting whom.

Managers

For decades, agents and managers coexisted in a delicate balance, each accommodating, if not loving, the other. All that changed in January 1999. It was then that Hollywood's most celebrated and oft-hated former agent Michael Ovitz suddenly returned from the dead—reincarnated as a manager. Worse, he retuned "stealing" managers and artists, the most celebrated being Rick and Julie Silverman Yorn, two of Hollywood's young managers, whom he talked into joining his newly formed Artists Management Group.

For years, managers were considered a "luxury" item, a paid friend to arrange travel and wardrobe, to hand-hold and play therapist, to watch out for a star's interests and to give career advice. Agents viewed them as life forms well down the Hollywood food chain, at best a useless hindrance between themselves and the client. Their specialty was perceived to be has-beens and wanna-bes, actors who needed hands-on career makeovers. Years ago, much of their clientele was young stand-up comedians like Steve Martin and Robin Williams who needed a boost off the lounge-act circuit. Managers countered that they could supply the personal guidance that agents were too busy to bother with. Managers charged that agents "sold" their clients into projects; managers built careers.

Despite the sniping, the fact is there were some very important distinctions between the two professions. Agents were licensed and supposedly overseen by the state. Managers were not. Agents could solicit work for their clients. Managers were prohibited by law from procuring work for their clients. They could advise their clients, they could recommend projects and deals, but they could not sell their clients to a producer, a studio or a network. Of course, the legal line was a fine, if not nearly invisible, one. Who was to say that if, for instance, powerful manager Brad Grey happened to discuss his client Adam Sandler while talking to a couple of Disney executives about the then-new project *The Waterboy* that that conversation constituted soliciting employment? Though there was grumbling by the agents, they continued to look the other way.

On the flip side, managers held a very important right that agents had long jealously coveted: they could produce or own a piece of their clients' work. Back in the 1950s, the Screen Actors Guild negotiated an agreement that banned agents from the right to own anything they negotiated for their clients. The only exception was the exemption given to Lew Wasserman's MCA by then-SAG president Ronald Reagan, a longtime friend of the agency head. With its Revue production unit, MCA could both represent its clients and produce the same TV shows they starred in. MCA, which became known as the "octopus," flourished until the Justice Department raided it in 1962 on antitrust violations and Wasserman was forced to shut down the agency side of the business, consolidating the entire business as Universal Pictures.

Ex-William Morris agent-turned-manager Bernie Brillstein was among the first managers to cash in on the loophole. In the early '80s, he delivered his *Saturday Night Live* clients John Belushi, Gilda Radner and Dan Aykroyd to Mike Ovitz at then-upstart CAA. In 1984, Brillstein was rewarded with a lucrative executive producer's credit on the CAA-package *Ghostbusters*, which Ovitz sold to his compatriot Frank Price at Columbia. Brillstein began routinely attaching himself to clients' projects, his biggest score being the moneymaking sitcom *Alf*. A decade later, he teamed with hot young manager Brad Grey to launch Brillstein-Grey, creating a powerhouse firm that both represented a Who's Who of big stars and produced and owned pieces of such TV hits as *Just Shoot Me* and *NewsRadio*, and feature films like *The Wedding Singer*.

In the '90s, stars increasingly began moving to managers. Brillstein-Grey boasted a prestigious client list headed by Sandler, Brad Pitt, Nicolas Cage, Garry Shandling, Gary Sinise and Courteney Cox Arquette. The industry's red-hot young managers Rick and Julie Yorn at Addis-Wechsler had Leonardo DiCaprio, Cameron Diaz and Claire Danes. Sharon Stone placed herself with Chuck Binder. For one thing, many actors appreciated the TLC they received from managers, who not only picked up the phone but genuinely seemed to care about their careers and personal happiness. Under Yorn at Addis-Wechsler, Brad Pitt's manager Cynthia Pitt would deal with anything from the star's wardrobe to what material would be best for his career. Longtime manager Phyllis Carlyle has been credited with single-handedly turning around Melanie Griffith's career after the one-hit teen queen dropped from sight, putting on 30 pounds and donning the torn jeans, Salvation Army-chic look. Carlyle got her to lose weight, bought her a new wardrobe, changed her makeup and "mommied" her back on track. She then built her career gradually, putting her in Brian De Palma's *Body Double*, then Jonathan Demme's *Something Wild* and, finally, her breakout role in Mike Nichols's *Working Girl*. But as much as the personal touch, superstars liked the breaks they got when it came to commission fees. Unlike agents, who despite package fees still mostly billed a 10 percent commission, managers would settle for the ownership or producer's fee they could negotiate from the studio in lieu of charging the standard 15 percent. In a $10 million deal, that was a savings of $1.5 million to the client.

Agents soon came to the real-ization it was better to do business with managers than fighting them and risk losing clients. CAA, in particular, began working closely with their clients' managers. The benefits of such a partnership were many. Managers were adept at advising on material and proved very helpful in following up on the personal details that an agent did not have time for and which became a sore point with many clients. Having the manager on the team also headed off the likelihood of him or her stealing the client. They also proved useful in deterring raids by rival agencies. But even more important, managers could deliver clients to the agents. Of course, there was the quid pro quo: managers expected the agents to deliver their clients to them.

Ovitz had built CAA into the industry's dominant agency through a tough, almost paranoid, us-against-them attitude in which all the old-style gentlemanly rules of conduct were quickly ground beneath the tank tread. The agency stole agents and clients mercilessly from rivals. It intimidated its own clients through the sheer force of its power. Controlling the industry's top directors and stars, it shoved expensive CAA packages down the throats of studio heads with a take-it-or-leave-it arrogance never before seen in a town known for its ruthlessness.

But Ovitz had taken a great fall. Overplaying his hand in negotiations with head Seagram heir Edgar Bronfman Jr.'s newly acquired Universal Studios, Ovitz blew the deal in 1995 and had to watch the job be handed to his second-in-command, CAA partner Ron Meyer. In a knee-jerk response, Ovitz jumped to Disney, where longtime friend and Disney chairman Michael Eisner had thrown him a rope as his heir-apparent. Ovitz failed miserably in the confines of the publicly held corporation. In 14 short months, he and Eisner had a bitter falling-out and Ovitz was sent packing with a $100 million stock-option severance—a Golden Finger, as some wags joked. Humiliated, with no place to go, Ovitz holed up out of view and licked his wounds.

There was speculation that Ovitz would try to start some kind of entertainment company. It was well known he had chafed under the 10 percent rule. He branched out into consulting for Coke, investing in supposedly cutting-edge sound-editing equipment, dabbled in corporate brokering with the Columbia sale to Sony, and then tried to find a buyer for Credit Lyonnaise-owned MGM/UA. Ovitz had complained bitterly that the only way to make real money and thus wield real power was through ownership. He had even toyed with schemes to set up a CAA-controlled production unit in Europe.

After reports of his suffering a depression, he resurfaced at the head of an investment group to buy Garth Drabinsky Livent Inc. theatrical company, which brought spectacle back to the stage with *Ragtime*, *Fosse* and *Show Boat*, but which, unhappily for Ovitz, turned out to be teetering on bankruptcy. He followed with a late bid to buy Polygram, which no one took seriously, then popped up with an elaborate plan to bring the NFL back to Los Angeles—specifically on the site of a former chemical dump in Carson, California. Hollywood, however, barely paid attention as Ovitz spent every waking hour romancing the steak-and-potato millionaire team owners who didn't know the difference between a film package and the one delivered by UPI—and didn't care.

Then suddenly Ovitz was back in the klieg lights. And with muscle. Two weeks after the announcement of the birth of AMG, Hollywood was hit with the news. Ovitz's onetime agency lieutenant Mike Menchel had left CAA to join AMG, taking his biggest client, Robin Williams, with him. Not even a month old, Ovitz's new company already fielded one of the industry's most impressive client lists: Leonardo DiCaprio, Claire Danes, Cameron Diaz, Robin Williams, Minnie Driver, Marisa Tomei. Ovitz quickly added former CAA client director Martin Scorsese. Soon Hollywood cellulars burned with rumors Ovitz was talking to longtime CAA agent Rick Nicita and his star client Tom Cruise. Not long after, CAA's Lee Gabler was leaving client David Letterman's office and ran face-to-face into Ovitz who had come for his own appointment with his former client. Rumors swirled that Ovitz was talking about launching some new kind of production unit in which both AMG and the clients could become producing partners. The gauntlet had been thrown down. Agents throughout Hollywood wailed that the former über-agent was bent on nothing less than world domination.

The fragile peace that existed between agents and managers was shattered. Both sides geared up for battle. CAA head Richard Lovett took the unprecedented move of prohibiting CAA clients from doing business with his former mentor. Those clients who already signed would be dropped. In the meantime, the town's agencies banded together to call for stricter enforcement of the rule prohibiting managers from procuring work and encroaching on their business. They threatened complaints with the state, demanding that managers be licensed as well as agents. They wanted the ownership rule to be revisited to level the playing field. Old Ovitz enemies like Brillstein and DreamWorks partner David Geffen began looking to undermine Ovitz. Privately, managers and agents began carving each other up to clients over lunches at industry watering holes.

It's a fight that shows no signs of letting up. In fact, with the studios playing hardball to cut costs and agents and managers battling each other, Hollywood in the new millennium may be one of the most exciting, if hazardous, theaters of duty in corporate America.

Entertainment Attorney

You won't find an actor going anyplace without two things: a comb and a lawyer. Attorneys may be among the town's least-known participants, but they are, nonetheless, among its richest and most powerful. Forget that a phrase like "off the top" or "break even" can have a different meaning on a different day on a different contract, the sheer sum of money involved in a single contract demands the services of a lawyer. With stars like Jim Carrey making upwards of $20 million per picture —more than many businesses make in an entire year—superstars are virtual minimoguls with their own production companies or incorporated businesses. The tax and other consequences of each negotiation are crucial. Though many agents can navigate their way through the complex numbers and bargaining points, some find themselves in way over their heads. That's where that most specialized of all animals comes in: the entertainment attorney.

Traditionally, attorneys charged extravagant fees for their "billable hours," but that seemed like chump change when they worked on a movie or television deal worth millions. In 1973, Tom Pollock, handling negotiations with agent Jeff Berg, haggled Universal into giving George Lucas 20 percent of the gross on *American Graffiti*, which ultimately made $67 million in domestic box office. Instead of charging Lucas a flat hourly rate, Pollock, following the lead of a new breed of entertainment attorneys, took five percent of the director's cut—$650,000. Pollock's deal was identical for *Star Wars*: five percent of the $40 million the director made from the gross of $250 million. By the time Pollock's deal became part of Hollywood lore, most of the boutique entertainment attorneys followed suit. In many cases, if the client didn't have an agent, the attorney fee rose to 10 percent. Other attorneys worked out other arrangements, such as charging an hourly rate plus a "deal making bonus."

Since the biggest entertainment attorneys know everyone in town on both sides, many clients elect to be represented by their attorney alone, rather than by an agent who charges 10 percent. Indeed, since attorneys are involved in the most intimate details of the business' biggest deals, they know what projects are in development or in need of casting. There is not a production veep in town who is not going to return a phone call from an entertainment attorney such as Bert Fields. ❱

Job Descriptions

EXAMPLE: "SHAKESPEARE IN LOVE"

above the line

PRODUCER Forget those tired cigar and casting-couch jokes, the producer is the single most pivotal entity on a film—the equivalent of the baseball manager or the newspaper editor in chief. He or she develops the project (from pitch or spec script to first draft to last), brings all the elements together (from director to actors to publicists), ferrying the film from concept to final print. He may have his own production company with a "first-look" deal at a studio (meaning the studio gets first crack at anything the producer develops) or the sweeter "housekeeping" deal (i.e., the studio supplies production offices, staff, development money, even trains, planes and leased Mercedes-Benzs). A-listers like Imagine Entertainment's Brian Grazer or Joel Silver at Warner Bros. pride themselves on finding their own projects, but studios with whom they have production deals also deliver to them their hottest material—say, the latest Michael Crichton novel—to develop.

Independent producers not associated with a major studio arrange for financing and the most successful—and powerful—maintain tight control of their projects from start to finish, overseeing not only the financial and technical aspects of production, but the postproduction process, distribution and marketing

PRODUCER

efforts as well. The best have a profound influence over the ultimate artistic work as well, something generally thought to be exclusively the director's bailiwick. The old joke is that everyone from the caterer to the star "really wants to direct." But directors know who's got the real power and—unless they're already one of the elite *auteurs* who do both—they really want to produce.

CO-PRODUCER

When there is one, the co-producer is invariably one of the big players on the project. Sometimes co-producers reflect the fact that the project is a joint venture of two or more production companies, each of which has placed its own exec on the project, or two producers have competing rights to a project, or a writer has enough clout to demand a producing credit in order to protect his or her work. Depending on who they are and how they got there, they normally function much like the producer, but usually under his or her command. Because of Hollywood dealmaking, the title is open to a multitude of interpretations. Whether "co-" or not, producers are paid large fees for their work on a movie, but the real money comes from the back end of the deal, where the chosen few even share in gross profits. (See "Let's Make a Deal".)

EXECUTIVE PRODUCER
Despite the title, the executive producer is rarely the individual who actually "makes" the movie. Often, the executive producer is the title given as an inducement to someone in control of a key element of a project, perhaps a writer who came up with the initial concept or an independent producer who controls the option to a book, script or screenplay upon which the project is based. Executive producers can be paid a fee (anywhere from $150,000 to even $1 million for a "hot" project) and share in profit participation—how many points, and whether they are net or gross, depends on how big the project and how big the executive producer. Often the executive producer is a talent manager who has sold his client in to a picture and taking a producer credit—and fee—as his cut of the deal.

ASSOCIATE PRODUCER
An associate producer can be a real producer or anyone (director, writer, favorite nephew) who has enough clout on a project to grab the credit. But no matter how the contract cuts it, associate producer is one of those above-the-line titles that usually carries with it real responsibilities, which range from giving notes on screenplay drafts to running interference with studio VPs to just running, period—mostly for the producer.

LINE PRODUCER

Aptly named, the line producer is on the producing line—and, more often than not, on the hook. Not considered a "creative" element, he or she is nonetheless an essential field colonel, the producer and director's right-hand man, overseeing the day-to-day operations of the production process, creating a shooting schedule, ensuring that the work proceeds according to said schedule on time and on budget, scheduling actors and crew for daily takes and generally dealing with all the life-and-death emergencies that explode on a set every two or three hours. One of the first hired and one of the first fired, especially when things go wrong (meaning behind schedule) and the "real" producers can't swallow deeply enough to fire the director.

The only member of the team who faces the ultimate challenge: the horror of the blank page. Where the director, like the conductor of a symphony orchestra, is essentially an interpretive artist, the screenwriter, akin to a composer, is a more purely creative artist. The screenplay is the verbal blueprint from which the visual creation is constructed. It it is also the original magnet that attracts top talent and funding to the project. Even when adapting material from a novel or play, the screenwriter must conceive the film's architecture and establish its authorial point of view. He or she draws characters the actors will bring to life; creates the words they will articulate; limns the world of the story to which the production designer and art director will give three-dimensional form. Many rewrites may be required before a final shooting script is settled upon. Sometimes a dizzying number of writers may be recruited to work on the story and characters or punch up the dialogue. Some screenwriters work full time as script doctors, reworking scripts for various studios without ever receiving credit. In many cases today, the screenwriter is also the director—the so-called "hyphenate," a dual credit pioneered by writer-directors like Preston Sturges or Billy Wilder. (Sturges, in fact, agreed to accept no director's fee for the first-time privilege of helming one of his own scripts.) Ultimately, however, it is the writer's vision which is brought to the screen and the "voice" he gives the movie, through plot, characterization and dialogue, that resonates in the final cut—though who and how many writers get credit for it is a process determined by the Writers Guild of America, often as mysterious as the act of creation itself.

DIRECTOR As head of the production unit, the director brings to a project its artistic vision. He translates the screenplay into a movie, bringing to bear all of the production's resources, including its cast and crew. Though film is by its nature a collaborative art, the director provides leadership; he makes the myriad decisions that shape what winds up on the screen. In preproduction, he works closely with the producer to engage key creative personnel, cast and crew. With the screenwriter, he refines and polishes the material. During shooting, he choreographs both the actors' and the camera's movements, developing a film's rhythm and visual style well before the editing process begins. In postproduction, the director works closely with the editor to resolve issues of pacing and structure. The director must combine creative finesse and technical know-how to tell a cogent and emotionally compelling story on film. Since a film's scenes are bound to be shot out of sequence for efficiency and economy, the director has got to maintain a sense of the whole; he must be capable at all times of seeing the bigger picture and somehow translating that vision to the lesser mortals around him. As overseer of a bewildering array of egos, he must also function as psychiatrist, referee, timekeeper and father-confessor. Finally, he is the ultimate keeper of a movie's vision, tone, look, feel, and emotional and psychological impact.

Job Descriptions

**DIRECTOR OF PHOTOGRAPHY /
CINEMATOGRAPHER**

The eyes and artistic soul-mate of the director, the DP transforms light into images. He is in charge of all camera operations, as well as the technical aspects of lighting and photographing the project. He assists the director in the choice of camera angles and setups and in obtaining the desired mood through lighting. He is responsible for the general composition of the scene, the colors of the images, the choices of cameras, lenses and filters and film stock; the setups and movements of the camera; and the integration of any special effects. The director's closest collaborator in the creative process, the DP through the choices he makes, can enhance characterization and clarify structure. The DP must not only capture action and dialogue in his work, but also the visual tone, the "look" of the movie. He must bring to life a picture of the film's deeper emotional and intellectual content. Though considered a craftsman, the DP may be the purest visual artist on the set.

CAMERA OPERATOR The camera operator is the person literally with his hands on the button, the guy you see on the dolly with his eye pressed to the viewfinder. He or she is the tech nerd who knows everything about cameras, from geared heads to ocular-diopter settings, and is responsible directly to the DP. He or she maintains the composition, focus and movement desired by the director of photography, ensures the quality of each shot, rejects any take that is deemed faulty, and is responsible for the proper functioning of his assigned camera. Ultimately, the DP is only as good as the camera operator rolling his film.

Think of *Gone With the Wind*, *The Godfather* or *Star Wars* without, respectively, Max Steiner's, Nino Rota's or John Williams's epic overtures—music that is as identified with the film as the stars' performances. Technically, a composer seeks to match the tone and style of the music to the thematic and dramatic needs of the film, helping to underscore the director's thematic vision. That would be but a mechanic's description to most film composers, however, especially the great ones, who consider themselves classicists in the tradition of Beethoven, Wagner, Stravinsky. Their musical compositions seek to capture not only the theme of the particular film but the human truths all great artists hope to reveal. Though the best film music adds immeasurably to the experience of a movie— often literally creating the action and mood of the story—the composer often does not begin work until the postproduction stage. Toiling under the gun—in fact, worse, under the anxious stares of the director and producer—he or she frequently may have only a week or two to do the work and will rarely have more than six weeks. The composer often records the score (sometimes as conductor or instrumentalist) near the end of postproduction. No wonder gifted composers are even more rare than gifted directors. They are also among the most underrated artists in the filmmaking process. Bernard Herrmann's contributions to many of the best Hitchcock films, such as *Psycho*, are the element most viewers unconsciously carry away with them, without ever knowing the composer's name.

The conductor, who is often the composer himself, assembles the orchestra and/or musicians, then interprets and conducts for live recording the composer's compositions and scores. The orchestra literally plays in front of a movie screen, matching the movements to the action in the film. The conductor must not only be an accomplished practitioner of his craft, but understand the movement of film, how cuts and changing scenes require simultaneous changes in the music. Like the composer, he or she must also understand the director's vision, the theme and emotional life of the film, creating a separate music dialogue to parallel the spoken dialogue of the script. Appropriately, in the beginning, music was the only "dialogue" heard in the theaters of film's Silent Era.

The music editor is one of the "creatives," a trained musician whose job is to select and edit the music tracks to maximize their cinematic impact. He or she reports to the supervising editor, but retains a good deal of freedom in marking the music cues in a scene, selecting the music (when it is "canned," or already published), even playing or recording piano sketches or other musical bites to be used. The music editor also monitors all recording sessions, checks the synchronization of the music with the dialogue and sound effects, and prepares cue sheets for dubbing purposes. In a sense, the music editor is a kind of frontline composer.

FILM EDITOR

The most unsung—and perhaps most ingenious—artisan in Hollywood, the film editor has saved many a potential bomb. Following the shooting script and in collaboration with the director, the editor selects, arranges and assembles the disparate shots, scenes and sequences of the film into a continuous whole and controls the synchronization of picture and sound. Often, even as a film continues in production, the editor is tentatively assembling the material into what will become the rough cut—the first edited version of the film composed of the best shots in the best arrangement. Slowly and painstakingly, the editor and director will continue to refine and shape the material to achieve the most effective flow, pacing and rhythm. Since film is a moving medium, there is no job more important. Film buffs like to point that out in the classic shower scene in Alfred Hitchcock's *Psycho*. Designed by Hitchcock himself, who made final editing decisions, those all-too-real, blood-curdling knife thrusts never even touched Janet Leigh's skin. The editor can emphasize patterns, themes or motifs suggested by the director, and by adding or subtracting just a beat or two in a scene, dramatically alter the impact of a performance. The editor's final version, from which the original negative is cut together and sent to the film lab along with the final sound mix, may comprise as much as one-fifth or as little as one-thirtieth or less of the total footage originally shot.

The assistant editor assists the film editor in a variety of technical tasks, including synchronizing film images and sound. Critically, he or she is responsible for the storing and processing of film materials and for keeping a record of all pieces of film—a job that has a very direct effect on the outcome, not to mention existence, of the finished product. Often, the assistant editor will also serve as a sort of quality assurance officer, carefully checking processed film when it is returned by the lab and overseeing maintenance of editing equipment.

CASTING DIRECTOR The casting director begins studying the script for a breakdown of what roles must be cast and clues as to the types of actors the screenwriter and director might have in mind. Since producers are notoriously known for reading scripts with a box-office name in mind, leading players are generally associated with the project from its inception and figure as above-the-line talent, their deals negotiated through the producer and, often, the director. But all other parts are the casting director's province. He or she will draw together a pool of talent suited to each role, screen each of the actors and then present a manageable range of choices to the director and producer for their consideration. The casting director may be called upon to consult on final picks, and may even negotiate contracts for the actors on behalf of the production company, but he or she is unlikely to make any really big decisions alone. On the other hand, not a few stars (Kevin Costner, for one) owe their careers to the discerning, creative eye of the casting director who can often identify raw talent to launch an actor's career, making the job a pivotal creative position.

PRODUCTION DESIGNER The production designer conceptualizes and brings to life the locale (or, often, many disparate locales) described by the action and setting of the story. Known on some projects as the art director, he creates the scene in the broadest possible sense, renders key elements of the production design, and ensures that the sets can accommodate not only the actors, but the camera, lighting and a crew that can easily comprise 50 to 100 technicians and craftspeople, too. He is the architect of the visual world of the film and the ways it resonates with respect to scale, period and tone. In addition to designing soundstage sets—from small rooms to huge ships in 100,000-gallon tanks of water—the production designer oversees other art department personnel (including props, costumes, hair and makeup), coordinates shoots on studio back lots and searches out locations. He is counted on by the director to maintain the accuracy and consistency of the film's art elements and their execution, ultimately to make the movie "picture perfect."

On productions such as *Shakespeare in Love*, the art director supervises all sets, model and prop construction and finishing, scenic artwork and set dressing, sometimes overseeing and hiring the set designer, scenic artist and sketch artists. The art director also works under the production designer to coordinate costuming, makeup and hairstyling with the makeup department. In preproduction, the art director analyzes the script visually and dramaturgically, determining the number and types of sets needed, and the overall look of the production design, from props and furniture to costumes and picture titles. For period pieces, the art director must do intensive research in order to re-create the styles and look of the particular era, ensuring historical accuracy. It wouldn't do, for instance, to have Shakespeare plop himself down on an imported Louis XVI loveseat, since Louis would not wear the crown of France for another 40 years after Will wrote *Romeo and Juliet*.

Working from the production designer's sketches, notes and specifications, the set designer produces the working plans from which the settings are constructed and oversees their fabrication, finishing and painting, acting as a kind of foreman for the various craftsmen, from painter to carpenters. As assistant to the production designer, whose concern is the overall look of the film, the set designer focuses a bit more narrowly on the look of the settings.

Though not listed in the *Shakespeare* credits, the scenic artist is a routine member of any art department, especially on a historical drama. He works with the art director and/or production designer to create all sets, noting and ordering all materials, paints and equipment needed to create backings, drops, cycloramas and mattes, as well as sketches to render the scene. He or she also supervises film tests of the scenic artwork to ensure that the look of the sets is both realistic and compelling.

COSTUME DESIGNER Working within the visual milieu established by the production designer, the costume designer designs the garments worn by all the actors in the film and oversees fabrication of the clothing. Depending on the subject and style of the movie, the costume designer may have to shop at thrift stores or couture designer boutiques for appropriate items. He or she may have to research historical tailoring and dressmaking techniques to achieve accuracy in a period movie. A "costume drama" like *Shakespeare in Love*, which requires a deep understanding of historical periods, their style, culture, trade and manufacturing, is also a showcase for the designer's art and, understandably, tends to be the sort of project with which designers long to be associated.

COSTUME MAKER The costume maker, also known in pre-PC times as the seamstress, is called in when costumes cannot be rented or purchased. The costume maker works closely with the art director and costume designer to assemble and sew both male and female attire to be used in the shoot, functioning much as a couture designer's head seamstress. He or she also does the tucks, letting-outs and other alterations marked by the cutter/fitters on all rented costumes to specifically fit the actors and actresses wearing the clothes.

There is super-sophisticated movie star glamour makeup, makeup intended to be unobtrusive and virtually invisible, and then there is monster makeup that defines the features of swamp dwellers, jungle beasts or space aliens. The makeup artist must have the skills to achieve all these effects as required by the particular project to which he or she is attached at the moment. He or she heads the makeup department and supervises application of makeup to the performers from forehead to feet. As the science of molding, animatronics and synthetic rubber advances, the makeup artist must not only have a creative eye but a sound knowledge of advancing technology. It's been a technological lifetime since the days of creating the gloppy eyelashes of Elizabeth Taylor's *Cleopatra* to the goo-dripping double jaws of the *Alien* monster.

SENIOR HAIRSTYLIST

The hairstylist determines the appropriate hairstyles for all characters in all scenes, working with the key makeup artists and overseeing the assistant hairdressers. Like music and costuming, a hairstylist can help create not only the look of a movie, but entire pop trends. Think what Keanu Reeves's closely cropped hair did for the image of law enforcement in *Speed* or Cuba Gooding Jr.'s dome in *Jerry Maguire* did for wide receivers.

PRODUCTION MANAGER Sometimes called "production supervisor," the production manager often shares or incorporates the responsibilities of the line producer. Basically, the job is about guaranteeing that the wishes of the director—great and small—are granted throughout the shooting of the film. Typically, the production manager does the breakdowns of the day's shooting and schedules the most efficient use of cast, crew, equipment and locations. Like the line producer, the job requires an intimate knowledge not only of the production process, but also the unwritten codes of the industry pecking order, especially in regards to running interference with big stars and sensitive creative types. He or she works closely with the first assistant director to expedite transportation, accommodations and meals, as well as hires additional production personnel if needed during shooting. Another vital lieutenant in the field, the production manager's duties—and fortunes—are tied to the requirements (and occasionally the whims) of the director.

ASSISTANT DIRECTOR Essentially a more administrative than creative role, the AD nonetheless provides crucial support to the director. The first assistant director usually coordinates the efforts of the cast and crew and maintains order on the set. He may be requested by the director to arrange crowd scenes and oversee background and atmospheric action. When so instructed by the director, the AD gives the order for the camera and sound personnel to begin recording the scene. The second assistant director is backup to the AD and also keeps the huge flow of paperwork generated during filming moving between various individuals and departments. He or she writes out the daily call sheets and production reports.

SECOND-UNIT DIRECTOR On large projects, a second film unit may be required to shoot action sequences and other stunts, a "cast of thousands," special effects or distant locations. It is helmed by the second-unit director who functions in the same manner as the director does in the unit engaged in principal photography. The work of the second-unit director must match and integrate with film shot by the director. Many times, the second-unit director is the first AD, getting a shot at finally running the camera instead of handling the crew and paperwork.

SUPERVISING SOUND EDITOR

The supervising sound editor oversees the design and building of all the sound tracks in preparation for the final mix of a film. He or she analyzes the script in preproduction for the total sound design, working closely with the director, music editor and picture editor to establish the "tone" the picture is to have. During production, the sound editor assembles, synchronizes and checks the quality of all tracks including dialogue, substitutes music and sound effects for the temp dub, and makes any necessary repairs or dubs.

The production sound mixer reports to the director and is in charge of recording and ensuring the quality of all sound, dialogue, special effects and incidental sound, on set or on location. He also works with the DP in placing the boom and other microphones, making sure not to encroach on lighting patterns or camera-frame limits. He or she has to break down the script, then analyze camera angles and coverage to plot out each scene for proper placement, overseeing the boom operator, sound technicians and recordists. The sound mixer is also responsible for notifying the AD about any extraneous noise on the set, making sure all vents, air conditioning, refrigerators, cell phones, beepers, etc. are turned off. The quality of the sound is the responsibility of the production mixer, which could make for a nice fall guy on the production. That is why he or she has the option to voice-slate "Under Protest" directly on the recording if any take is recorded over his or her objection. More politic mixers, however, find a way to convey their feelings more informally to the director.

The sound recordist works under the direction of the production mixer to record on a separate tape recorder production sound—for example, the sounds of the "live" audience at the premiere performance of *Romeo and Juliet.*

DIALOGUE EDITOR The dialogue editor's job is basically to replace all the dialogue and background voices that don't work. They can be too flat, too garbled, too understated, too overstated, drowned out by noise (that stupid Doberman down the street on location who wouldn't stop barking). The dialogue editor prepares the new dubs for looping by the foley mixer (*see below*) and the director. He or she has to know to the precise frame where the replacement dialogue goes, otherwise the scene will look like something straight out of a Hong Kong karate movie dubbed in English.

FOLEY EDITOR The foley editor oversees all sound effects, working with the foley artists and foley mixer. He or she analyzes the script, marking needs for sound effects in each shot, scene or sequence, schedules foley sessions and is responsible for selecting and accurately placing the sound effects in each shot, along with canned and production recorded sound effects.

FOLEY ARTIST

A fancy name for the sound-effects genius, the foley artist creates all the sound effects for a movie, from explosions and drooling retractable alien teeth to clapping thunder and the sound of footsteps running (anyone who saw Albert Brooks's *Modern Romance* will recall the hilarious scene of his sound editor character calling up the track of "the Hulk running" to double for the heavy footfalls of a space station crewman clomping down a corridor). A foley artist uses canned sounds, tape, live sound and re-created effects—many times holing up in a room filled with gizmos from sheets of galvanized aluminum (thunder) and boxes of sand (walking) to Cracker Jacks (which create a sound only a foley fully understands).

FOLEY MIXER

The foley mixer works under the director and foley editor and records all sound effects created by the foley artists, selecting and placing microphones, supervising the patching of the control panel, maintaining modulation and filtering controls, and working with the projectionist to ensure reel sequence—in short, ensuring the quality and accuracy of all sound effects in the film. No matter whether the sound is as subtle as the plop of a fly hitting a trout stream in *A River Runs Through It* or as ear-splitting as a Tie-fighter in *Star Wars*, a false note by a foley is as fatal to a scene as a blown line by a leading man.

BOOM OPERATOR

The boom operator is in charge of those long fishing pole microphones that have become as familiar as directors' chairs in any movie that has a scene showing a film being shot. But there is a reason for those booms: fitted with sophisticated microphones, they can be kept out of camera frame during shooting while still being sensitive enough to pick up the tenderest whisper by an actor in a love scene. But the boom operator is not limited to the boom: he or she also is in charge of a variety of state-of-the-art mikes, from shotgun mikes to parabolic microphone which can pick up sounds from great distances (just ask any CIA listening station). Besides setting all mikes out of sight of the camera—but within earshot of the actors—the boom operator also has to memorize each piece of dialogue by each actor in a shot in order to know where to move the boom to pick up the actor's line, all the while following the camera action on a small television monitor.

RERECORDING MIXER

He or she works in the postproduction phase to assemble and mix dialogue, music and sound effects tracks, following a videotape of the director's cut. The rerecording mixer supervises the patching of input from dummy room to dialogue elements, then oversees the final mix with the producer, director, music and sound effects rerecording mixers, finally mastering for release in three digital formats—Dolby, Digital Theater System and Sony Dynamic Digital System, plus a two-track backup. In short, what you hear at the theater is what the mixers get to you.

In many cases the master magician, the supervisor is in charge of overseeing all special effects personnel and all the effects in a film, from very high-tech digital work to the blowing up of a building to simply creating shadows where there are none. The special effects supervisor designs, constructs, prepares and rigs all firearms, explosives, incendiaries, man-made rain, floods, wind, dust, smoke, mechanical gags (a specific effect in a scene), flying spaceships and just about everything else a screenwriter's imagination cooks up. These days, he or she will work also with outside special effects companies like George Lucas's Industrial Light & Magic (ILM), which creates envelope-pushing, computer-generated visuals, from the dinos in *Jurassic Park* to characters like Jar Jar Binks in *The Phantom Menace* who do not fully exist outside a computer chip. Other effects masters, like the legendary Stan Winston, specialize in creating monsters. But it is the job of the special effects supervisor to oversee all the bells and whistles, to make sure they meet the director's expectations and that they all go off safely, without a hitch. Specialists under his or her command range from the armorer, who handles weaponry, to the powder technicians, who set off the explosions, to the atmospheric technicians, who make it snow in Hollywood in July.

GAFFER

As the head electrician, the gaffer oversees all the lighting needs, working closely with the DP to create the right tone for each scene. The gaffer supplies all the lighting mechanics: luminaries, gloves, stands, mounting devices, connectors, power sources, scrims, diffusion gels and the like. He or she takes a post next to the DP during rehearsals and shooting to modify any lighting techniques, overseeing the lighting crew, including the best boys (lighting technicians), riggers and special operators.

BEST BOY

There is no one best boy. The term means second in command. Thus, there is a best boy gaffer and a best boy grip. Under the gaffer, he or she is the assistant chief lighting technician, responsible for helping with the rigging, moving all the lighting equipment, checking each lamp, all the filters, gels, snoot assemblies, pipe grids, etc. And, of course, keeping all those miles of electrical cable coiled and out of the way of the fully insured box-office stars.

KEY GRIP

The Bekins man of the industry, the grip is in charge of moving any equipment that does not have a plug on it, like foils and dollies, and for safely preparing the set. He works closely with the DP to expedite the lighting, camera placement and camera movement procedures and pretty much grunts all that tonnage from truck to set and back again.

Yes, there really is a person who holds that familiar slate, bangs the clapper bar and announces to the camera, "Scene One, Take Two." Though frequently two separate jobs, the clapper and the loader responsibilities often overlap and are combined, depending on the production. The clapper, in fact, is the second assistant camera operator whose job is, among other things, keeping track of each take, noting on the slate the production company, production title, director, cinematographer, date and take number so that the editor has a road map to follow when assembling the rough cut; ensuring that every camera is in working order and placed according to the DP's wishes to cover every angle in a shot; and assisting the DP and camera operator before, during and after takes, from running for refreshments to just running. The loader is responsible for handling the film, properly loading and downloading all film magazines, keeping dead-accurate records of all exposed and unexposed film and, ultimately, delivering the film to the producer or designated company representative for film processing. The job may seem deceivingly simple, but imagine what would happen to, say, a Quentin Tarantino movie if the film magazines were incorrectly marked, logged out of sequence or lost— something akin to knocking over a Scrabble board just as the last tile was played.

SCRIPT SUPERVISOR

The script supervisor works with the director to keep precise notes on every shot, scene and change of dialogue and action before and during production. Part of the artistic process is spontaneous creativity: a director midway through a scene sees a better way to play it, the actor dislikes a line and improvises his or her own which is far superior to the one in the shooting script, or, more than likely, the actor simply mistakes the written line and speaks a new and more natural and dramatic line that more truly reflects his or her character. It is the script supervisor's responsibility to note the change in the shooting script and notify the director and the picture editor of the change and to ensure continuity with any following scenes, which could be shot days later. Similarly, he or she records everything that happens in a frame, including actor positions and distances from the camera, the placement of cameras, the use of handheld cameras, the T-stop and any filtering of the lens, prop and set dressing conditions, and any comments by the director concerning the take. Working closely with the script supervisor is a continuity girl (or boy) whose sole job is to ensure that each take matches the subsequent take, even though a single shot may have as many as 20 separate takes and could be filmed on different days. This has made for great sport with film trivia buffs, who love to point out continuity gaffes—a leading man, say, who's wearing a hat in a scene, then a second later, the hat is magically gone, then a second after that, like something out of Penn & Teller, the hat is back on his head. It is a sure sign someone forgot to properly annotate the shooting script and keep track of the takes.

STUNT COORDINATOR The stunt coordinator works under the director, planning, staging and executing all the stunts in a scene, whether they're to be performed by the actors themselves or the specially trained stunt crew—experts in stunt driving, fighting, falling, flying, sword-fighting and anything else that requires a special physical skill and involves risk. The stunt coordinator works closely with the special effects technician to plan, execute and ensure the safety of each stunt, whether it's pretending to be hit by a bullet or falling off a 40-story building onto a collapsible airbag. Though rare, most fatalities on a set are going to be the stuntman. It's easy to spot stuntmen on any shoot: they are the last true American cowboys.

SCULPTOR While this may seem an esoteric job, a keen eye can spot a sculptor's handiwork in many a movie, especially a period piece like *Shakespeare in Love*, whose Tudor mansions showcased a good deal of pricey (albeit faux) statuary. The sculptor works under the set decorator and does exactly what the title suggests—sculpts artwork for the film. He or she is a trained sculptor—usually a university graduate—and is responsible for acquiring or sculpting any statuary required in a script. The Elizabethan-era *Shakespeare in Love* was a sculptor's dream job, re-creating Renaissance art that graced the mansions of the dukes and duchesses and the theaters of the day.

CARPENTER

The carpenter is part of the construction crew used to design and build all sets for a shoot which cannot be found on location. The carpenter does the framing, joisting and woodwork required to build any set from the ground up—most notably in the case of *Shakespeare in Love*, when the craftsmen created an entire Elizabethan theater: stage, seating, proscenium and all. The carpenter is just one of many craftsman, including woodcarvers, bricklayers, finishers, painters, masons, metal workers, welders, pipe fitters and electricians who re-create reality for the film, sometimes building entire edifices which could actually function.

STORYBOARD ARTIST

Long before the cameras are loaded, or the cast is cast, the storyboard artist sketches out the entire movie, especially complicated action sequences, scene by scene, illustrating what the major shots will look like, and helping the director and the DP to visualize what the film will look like. The process stimulates new ideas and points out which scene may not be fully conceptualized.

The wrangler is responsible for handling all the animals in a film—usually horses. He arranges for transportation of the animals, the necessary harnesses, wagons, saddles and equipment, leads the animals on-set, handles them between takes, as well as ensuring they have proper stabling and food. Things get tricky when the animals are cows, goats, chickens, snakes and iguanas, requiring knowledgeable people familiar with each set of animals. These days wranglers also work closely with the Humane Society to ensure that all animals are treated in accordance with prevailing laws and codes of humane treatment.

BABY WRANGLERS Baby wranglers—usually women and/or nurses—handle all babies or toddlers called for in a shot, subbing for their mothers and keeping their very temperamental stars as calm and winsome as humanly possible. The baby wrangler ensures that the diminutive star smiles or coos on cue, even though it is in the arms or staring into the unknown face of some strange actor—all the while making sure she herself stays out of frame. This may be the most unsung job in the entire crew.

television

Just as the studios inhabit the top of the film food chain, so too do the TV networks similarly dominate the television business. For nearly half a century, only three networks controlled the entire industry: the so-called Big Three: CBS, NBC and ABC. They were the first companies to rush to fill the American public's insatiable appetite for new fare from the brave new world of the small screen, which overnight revolutionized entertainment in the post-World War II years. The big agencies, William Morris and MCA, scrambled to transform their once-languishing radio and vaudeville stars into popular new TV personalities, helping the fledgling networks fill a void in programming.

That erstwhile world order began to crumble in the '90s, with the proliferation of cable, the Internet and new networks, which poached both the Big Three's audience and its cash cow—advertisers, who now had a far wider choice when it came to spending their clients' dollars. A simultaneous plunge in network viewership, fragmentation of marketable audiences, the gobbling-up of studios and networks by global-entertainment giants, plus skyrocketing production costs for new shows have all further shattered a highly structured, almost feudal empire into a chaotic turf war between an expanding number of players, where the rules of engagement change daily.

It could be said that in a real sense the television business was changed inexorably because of two men: Barry Diller and Rupert Murdoch. The former head of Paramount, Diller had left the studio in 1984 to run newly purchased Twentieth Century Fox. But instead of concentrating on building up Fox's feature division, Murdoch and Diller, to the disbelief and even ridicule of the industry, set about to create a fourth network, the Fox Broadcasting Company. Through a series of buyouts, Murdoch and Diller quickly turned a patchwork of TV stations and independents into Fox affiliates. Initially, the strategy was to broadcast Fox-owned programming a few nights a week, then gradually extend FBC programming to seven days a week.

Networks had been proscribed from owning their own programming since the passage of the Financial Interest and Syndication Rules, known as "Fin/Syn," in 1970. But, to the consternation of the Big Three, Fox argued successfully that FBC did not program full time as did CBS, NBC and ABC and, therefore, was not a "full" network subject to the rules.

Diller knew that competing head-to-head with the other networks in traditional programming would be prohibitively expensive and risky. Niche marketing—that is, targeting programming and advertising to a smaller and defined demographic in order to saturate that market rather than shotgunning an entire audience—was proving an increasingly popular and effective means of stretching a client's advertising dollars. Diller and Fox took the practice one step further: niche networking. FBC went almost exclusively after the free-spending 18- to 34-year-old urban male, a demographic coveted by beverage, clothing, electronics, automotive and snack food companies, to name just a few.

The network hit phenomenal pay dirt with the adult-oriented, animated breakout *The Simpsons*, which put Fox on the radar. The network aggressively went after NFL football, outbidding the sport's longest broadcasting partner CBS and shocking the entire industry. FBC used its NFL spots to promote a lineup of hip, edgy dramas and comedies, interspersed with low-budget reality programming. The network expanded to full-time programming and created critical and popular hits that included *The X-Files*, *Party of Five*, *Ally McBeal*, *King of the Hill* and *That '70s Show*. Though the shows were not Top 10 in the Nielsens, the traditional benchmark of ratings success, they nonetheless scored among the top programs watched by twenty- and thirty-somethings, attracting a loyal core audience and big-dollar advertisers. Diller would leave to form his own fledgling entertainment empire after just a few years, buying the TV marketer Home Shopping Network (and by the end of the '90s, adding the USA Network and Universal's TV production interests), but the mogul had set in motion the accomplishment of what no one thought possible: a viable fourth network.

The other studios soon followed Fox's lead, looking for a network to broadcast studio-produced programming. Time Warner founded the WB Television Network, whose mascot was the top-hatted Looney Tunes frog, which seemed to sum up the network's programming strategy: corner the youth market and create a hip, word-of-mouth buzz among urban teens. WB then moved to tie in with the film side of the youth market that was concurrently scoring box-office hits with such ensemble teen dramas as *Scream, I Know What You Did Last Summer*, and, later, *She's All That, Varsity Blues* and *Cruel Intentions*. The network, to this end, cut crossover deals with hot young screenwriter Kevin (*Scream, I Know What You Did*) Williamson, to create *Dawson's Creek* and writer Joss (*Buffy the Vampire Slayer*) Whedon to reprise his vampire blockbuster for the small screen.

UPN, co-owned by Paramount parent company Viacom and Chicago-based Tribune Company, has not been as successful. The fledgling baby net launched itself with the *Star Trek* franchise, *Star Trek: Voyager* and *Star Trek: Deep Space Nine*, which drew in a loyal audience of Trekkies. But the network's lineup of urban programming and its jump into animation with *Dilbert* was not successful. After changing direction this season, the network's viewership dropped 47 percent.

Meanwhile, the cable networks also competed for a slice of the viewership pie. Basic cable networks like USA, Lifetime, the Comedy Channel, E! and MTV, to name a few, vie for both audience share and advertising dollars. Pay networks like HBO, Showtime, Cinemax, the Movie Channel and Disney compete directly for viewership. In the past two decades, the cables transformed the dynamics of the network TV business, wiping out a valuable cornerstone of "event" programming. No longer could the networks use the cachet of premiering blockbuster movies on the small screen, programming they counted on not only to garner big Nielsens, but also to lend prestige to the entire network. At one time, a megahit like Steven Spielberg's *The Lost World: Jurassic Park* would have been used to anchor the fall season, delivering to the network a large audience to promote its new season schedule. By the '90s, however, a movie like *The Lost World: Jurassic Park* would already have run on cable scores of times before it ever got around to being slotted in amongst the advertising clutter of "free" TV.

Time Warner's cable unit, Home Box Office, or HBO, paved the way for the cable stations early on, striking exclusive deals not only with Warner Bros. and other studios to broadcast feature films before they were even released to video. Showtime soon followed. The cable channels next upped the ante by producing their own movies, notably HBO's *Barbarians at the Gate* and *The Late Shift*. They then took on the networks directly, producing edgy one-hour dramas and sexy comedies which, exempt from the censorship regimen imposed on the Big Three networks, were able

The TV business, like the film business, has a storied history of imaginative deal making aimed at attaching the hottest talent and hottest hits to a particular studio. Popular is the "overall deal," or development deal, in which a studio or large production company commits money (from hundreds of thousands of dollars into the millions) for the exclusive services of a writer or a producer for a certain number of years. This includes an office, support staff, development costs and expenses with the understanding that all material must be brought to the studio first. The talent will develop their own projects, but may also be asked to participate in projects at the stu-

dio. Take, for instance, a writer that is paid $500,000 a year under an overall deal with Twentieth Century Fox. The studio may need the writer to consult on *Two Guys and a Girl*. The studio will then charge, say, $20,000 per episode as a consulting fee to the show as part of the writer's half-million-dollar paycheck.

The holding deal is for someone the studio wants to be in business with, usually an actor or actress. This is an exclusive deal, structured with a certain time frame in mind (presumably a year, with an option for another) to find a proper vehicle for this person. An office is not provided. After generating some heat in *Townies*, (Molly Ringwald's ill-fated comeback vehicle), actress Jenna

to push the envelope of taste, subject matter and language. Early successes were HBO's talk show spoof, *The Larry Sanders Show*, a crossover critical and ratings success. More recently, HBO experienced successes with *The Sopranos*, *Sex and the City* and *Arli$$*, while Showtime scored its own hits with sci-fi programming such as *Stargate SG-1*, *The Outer Limits* and *Total Recall 2070*.

Meanwhile, basic cable networks also began producing

Elfman's managers shopped her around in an effort to find the of-the-moment starlet a "home." She eventually entered into a holding deal with Twentieth Century Fox, which set up a lunch for Elfman with *Grace Under Fire* and *Cybill* producers Chuck Lorre and Dottie Dartland. The three clicked and the concept for *Dharma & Greg* was born. Twentieth Century Fox took the idea and elements (Elfman, Lorre and Dartland) and pitched to all the networks in town. ABC stepped up to the plate with the most cash and a generous episode commitment.

The housekeeping deal, generally for non-writing producers and TV-movie producers, is a bare-bones version of the overall deal with no salary. Money will come when a project falls into place. Office space, assistant and expenses are covered, basically just enough to keep someone in the "stable" and ensure first right of refusal. Below the housekeeping deal is the if-come deal, a studio deal made with a writer or producer before an idea or concept is shopped to a network and contingent on the project selling. There is also the "vanity deal," a somewhat disparaging term for an overall deal with a hot actor or actress when there is no real expectation from the studio that anything will be generated, but it wants to be associated with this particular name. ▶

their own programming, in addition to showing syndicated reruns of former Big Three network shows and sports events. Barry Diller's USA network, encompassing Universal's television production unit, produced both made-for-TV movies and weekly shows including *Law & Order, Hercules: The Legendary Journeys* and *Xena: Warrior Princess*. The onetime music-video channel, MTV, went after the established network's youth audience, with such

The William Morris Agency came up with the concept of "packaging" back in the earliest days of television. Packaging essentially involves putting two or more elements together to sell a project to a network. Generally, a writer or "show-runner" is paired with a director or actor. The package is then sold to the network and the agency, instead of collecting 10 percent of its clients' salaries, charges a percentage of the licensing fee. WMA came up with the 5/5/10 formula, which involved 5 percent as the base license fee, 5 percent as deferred profits and 10 percent adjusted gross, meaning back-end profits when the show goes into syndication.

Being the pioneers that they were, WMA really functioned like a producer in the early days of packaging, not only combining all the elements, but also attaining corporate sponsors for their packaged shows. In later years, to be competitive, ICM and CAA entered the game with a 3/3/10 formula. Today, they may try for the 5/5/10 ratio, but have not been as successful as WMA in receiving that formula. Clients of an agency benefit from packages twofold—they do not pay commission on these deals and more job opportunities are created as a result.

The '80s saw packages derived out of just one element, more common than not a big-name actor, but these days, unless a party has considerable leverage, it is getting increasingly difficult for agencies to attain packaging fees for delivering just one player. Typically, agencies will only get fees for delivering multiple elements.

Split fees is an inevitable trend in packaging. For instance, on a particular deal, there can be a producer with an overall deal and talent with a holding deal at the same studio. However, the parties are represented by different agencies and then throw in a manager/ obligatory producer into the mix and things get confusing! The producer and the actor are supportive of the package because they don't have the agency taking their 10 percent, but the agencies and management/ production company must split a packaging fee if the project is to move forward.

Crossover from the feature community has taken packaging in

a new direction. Whether it's a feature director attached to direct a TV pilot that makes a package more enticing or its feature players flush with syndication fever, many who originally snubbed TV are jumping into the lucrative medium. Steven Spielberg was first with an executive producer credit on *ER* and many others have followed. Heavy hitters in the feature multimillion-dollar development deals: Joss Whedon, writer of *Buffy the Vampire Slayer* and *Toy Story*, created the TV series *Buffy the Vampire Slayer* as well as the spin-off, *Angel*. J.J. Abrams, writer of *Regarding Henry* and *Armageddon*, created *Felicity*, while Aaron Sorkin, who penned *A Few Good Men* and *The American President*, crossed over to create *Sports Night*. ▶

hip, alternative programming as the animated cult favorite *Beavis and Butt-head* and reality programming like *The Real World*. Even a seemingly niche channel as Comedy Central scored huge youth-market ratings with *South Park* and *Win Ben Stein's Money*.

Exhibiting the sincerest form of flattery—or desperation—the networks rushed into production their own edgy-youth knockoffs, most notably ABC's fall offering *Wasteland* by teen-soap guru Williamson. Increasingly, prime-time slots have been taken over by such copycat fare dominated by young, white urban ensemble casts à la *Party of Five*, *Buffy*, *Dawson's Creek*, *Felicity* and the cable entry *Sex and the City*. In fact, TV's fixation with the white urban troubled teen stirred a controversy in 1999. Minority groups erupted in protest when the networks previewed a fall lineup of copycat ensemble shows cast entirely with young white actors and actresses. The networks vehemently denied pandering to a young, white audience, but nonetheless sent panicked word back to their show creators requesting they quickly add minority characters to their respective programs. In addition, network executives sent word down the pipeline they were interested in seeing projects developed with minority themes or casting.

The minority issue was just the latest headache for the Big Three networks. They faced a host of other problems, ranging from the mini-net competition, declining audiences and shrinking ad revenues to in-house creative and organizational problems. Five years after its purchase of Capital Cities/ABC, the Walt Disney Company was still trying to digest the network it purchased in 1995. Like Fox, Disney wanted a network partner to broadcast its own programming. Disney chair Michael Eisner, who decades before had been in charge of ABC's Saturday morning programs, quickly found an outlet for the studio's animated shows with its *One Saturday Morning* lineup of children's programming. But the company struggled in prime time. Without the luxury of targeting a niche market, ABC searched for a hit to capture a sizeable chunk of the younger end of the traditional 18- to 49-year-old prime-time audience, hoping for a ratings winner it could then build a night of programming around, as NBC had with *Cheers*, followed by *Seinfeld* and then *Friends*. Though the network garnered respectable ratings with Michael J. Fox's *Spin City*, *Dharma & Greg* and even *Two Guys and a Girl*, they were far from franchise makers. Other than *Monday Night Football*, the network struggled for an identity, never really recovering from the loss of *Roseanne* a half decade earlier. The network's floundering ratings contributed to Disney's sagging stock price, which in two years had dumped 47 percent. In a cost-cutting move, the company folded its television production division into ABC in 1999. In a preview of things to come, perhaps, the network pulled a "If you can't beat 'em, join 'em move" hiring Kevin Williamson and putting their hopes in *Wasteland*.

The onetime "Tiffany Network," now encompassing the Westinghouse Broadcasting stations, CBS also has struggled, especially since its bread-and-butter programming had been the 50-plus viewership it dominated with family-oriented shows like the long-running *Murder, She Wrote*; *60 Minutes*; *Matlock* and, more recently, *Touched by an Angel*. The network suffered another setback when it lost NFL broadcasting to Fox. Hoping to shake its old-fogey image, CBS tried to lure younger viewers with a youth-oriented lineup in 1995. That experiment failed miserably. After a very public battle, CBS signed David Letterman to go head-to-head with Jay Leno in what became known as the Late Night Wars. CBS had hoped Letterman would not only win the late-night time slot but also lend the network a younger, edgier image. Instead, Letterman began losing the ratings battle with Leno. After bidding itself back into the NFL in 1998, the network has fallen back on its old reliables, using its NFL broadcasts to launch programming targeted at men. This combo has proved somewhat successful, giving it a boost in the ratings race with hits like *Everyone Loves Raymond* and the military-courtroom drama *JAG*, which CBS took from NBC.

NBC has continued to be the most successful of the networks, boasting flagship hits *ER*, *Friends*, and *Frasier*, as well as NBA games. It weathered the loss of its number-one rated show, *Seinfeld*, especially with ratings winners

Suddenly Susan and *Just Shoot Me*. Like the other networks, however, NBC, owned by the General Electric Company, has faced declining profit margins and shrinking audiences and continues frequently to be the subject of takeover rumors.

■ ■ ■

Behind the entertainment conglomerates' aggressive move into the broadcasting end of the television business was a Richter-rocking change in the 1990s in the rules that had governed the economic landscape of the industry since its earliest days. Codified in 1970 into the Financial Interest and Syndication Rules, or "Fin/Syn," the Federal antitrust rules strictly prohibited the networks from owning the shows they ordered and subsequently broadcasted only the studios and the production companies were allowed ownership of the product. Likewise, Guild and Federal laws prohibited talent agencies from producing or owning shows. The sole—and glaring—exception for years was a Screen Actor's Guild waiver given in the 1950s to Lew Wasserman's MCA by then-SAG president Ronald Reagan, Wasserman's longtime friend and client. Unprecedented, the waiver allowed the MCA's production wing, Revue Productions, to produce and own the shows the agency packaged to the networks for its clients. The arrangement ended in 1962, when the Justice Department raided MCA's offices on antitrust violations, prompting Wasserman to quickly shutter his renowned agency and, overnight, transformed MCA solely into a production entity as the parent of Universal Pictures.

Under the "Fin/Syn" rules, the studios were the production arm of the television industry—creating, casting, shooting and, most importantly, owning the sitcoms and dramas which composed the networks' season lineups. The relationship was much like that between the producer and studios in the film industry: the producers pitched, conceptualized and produced the programming; the networks did the greenlighting, had a major say in both creative and casting decisions and paid for the shows.

The networks paid the studios or the production company a licensing fee to broadcast their shows. The licensing fee was supposed to cover the budget of each episode of the show, including talent and crew salaries, production costs, overhead and the like. In reality, the licensing fee rarely covered actual costs, especially when the studio factored in its own prodigious overhead, insurance, interest payments and such. But as production costs skyrocketed in the 1980s and 1990s, with stars of hit shows commanding $1 million an episode, the licensing fees came nowhere near covering production costs—let alone making a profit for the studios. The gap between costs and fees grew to Grand Canyon proportions as the networks, hit by shrinking audiences and, thus, dwindling advertising fees, dug in to hold costs down, while the actual production costs raged out of control.

The result was that the studios were forced to deficit-finance their shows. Even hit shows like *Seinfeld* could put the studio hundreds of thousands of dollars in the red for each episode. To recoup their costs (and losses) the studios waited to see their profits on syndication fees. After four years the studios took over their ownership rights and were able to cut separate syndication deals both nationally and internationally that could make them hundreds of millions of dollars. But the show had to be a hit. No one could possibly know at the time a network ordered up episodes of a new show if the studio would have a hit series in its stable, and thus a syndication jackpot four years down the line. The studios simply had to roll the dice.

By 1991, Fox's ability to produce its own shows by claiming it was not a "real" network had already begun to undermine the authority of "Fin/Syn." The other mininets began to claim the same exemptions. The Big Three networks complained, with good justification, that they were being unfairly singled out, excluded from owning their own shows while the competition had a free hand producing and broadcasting its in-house product. Finally, in 1995, networks gained the full repeal of Fin/Syn. For the first time ever, the television industry became a open marketplace, peculiarly fertile ground for these new entertainment giants with both production and broadcasting capacities.

Within a few short years every network would have a sister studio or production entity producing in-house shows. Disney bought its own network ABC; Fox, and, later, Warner Bros., began their own broadcast networks. In September 1999, Sumner Redstone's Viacom pulled of perhaps the last megadeal of the millennium, purchasing the historical crown jewel of television, CBS, the network of Edward R. Murrow and Walter Cronkite, of *All in the Family* and *60 Minutes* and catapulting Viacom and Paramount into the super-heavyweight ring with Time Warner and Disney. At the time this book went to press, NBC remained the last belle at the ball. Immediately, rumors followed that Universal, with or without the participation of Barry Diller, would make a run at the last of the

Big Three. Corporations owned their shows from broadcast to syndication, maximizing profits and, at least on paper, guaranteeing favorable time slots for their projects.

Inevitably, such potential for conflicts of interest stirred controversy among many in the industry. Critics charged that networks would naturally favor shows produced by their sister studios when ordering up season pilots and scheduling the all-important time slots. Some pointed to NBC's undying support of the failed show *Union Square* a few seasons back. The show fared poorly both with critics and audiences, but NBC nonetheless slotted it into its Thursday night "must-see" lineup, where it eventually died anyway despite the leg up.

■　■　■

Whether produced by sister studios or independent creators, the television business still starts with that most celebrated of all industry rituals: the pitch. The pitch season for the following year begins more or less after the July 4th weekend. A quick overview of the concept of the show by its creator, the pitch lasts anywhere from 10 minutes to an hour, depending on how receptive the studio executive is. Typically it begins with a simple sentence or one-liner that sums up the premise of the project. For a half-hour show, it normally begins with an idea for a cold open (the scene before the opening credits), then fleshes out the important story beats, the act break and any emotional turns driving the story. The best pitches close with the tag, the final scene that runs before or during the closing credits.

The conventional wisdom says to pitch to the studio first and then shop for a network. However, A-list creators more than likely will start at the network level. *The X-Files'* Chris Carter and *Ally McBeal's* David E. Kelley, for instance, are known to take their projects directly to the director of network programming. Established producers or credited writers, on the other hand, will meet with a network vice president first. Lower-level writers start with the developmental and junior executives. If they like the premise, they send it up the managerial food chain.

TV's hottest talent sometimes can skip the whole pro cess. For instance, *Just Shoot Me* creator Steve Levitan, whose NBC deal was coming to a close, never even got around to pitching. Anxious to keep him on board, NBC offered him a preemptory multimillion-dollar deal, committing to a 13-episode order and a top time slot for whatever project he could come up with next. Twentieth Century Fox then set the writer/creator up with a lucrative studio deal on its lot. The result: both NBC and Twentieth Century Fox came out winners when Levitan landed on the concept for *Stark Raving Mad*. ∎

Job Descriptions

above the line

CREATOR

As with film, the "Above the Line" creative credits are all negotiated. As the title says, the creator is the person—usually an established producer, director or writer hyphenate—who created the show, whether it be a half-hour sitcom or one-hour drama. The person around whom an agency usually packages a show, the creator not only comes up with the original concept of the show but is instrumental in creating the story, the characters and the setting. The show's creator is likely to make the deal with the studio and network and almost always has an executive producer credit, even if he or she is not the actual show-runner. With series like *Seinfeld* and *Roseanne* syndicating for hundreds of millions of dollars, successful creators are as rare and valuable as a good TV show.

EXECUTIVE PRODUCER Unlike the film credit, the TV executive producer is the most important single person on a show, and often the creator himself. Chris Carter, David E. Kelley, Steven Bochco, are all creator/executive producers. Known as "showrunners," they do exactly that—run the show from the creative end, hiring the writers, story editors and cast. Equally important, they are the head writers who create the "feel" of the show and determine the final word on what story lines appear.

PRODUCER The producer is a top-level writer who is directly responsible to the executive producer and more often than not oversees the writing team, from first drafts to finished scripts.

A fancy title for writers with experience. Each episode has a separate "written by" credit. The writer is always someone from the writing staff, from lowest level to highest—staff writer/story editor, co-producer, producer, executive producer. Each show, however, must freelance out two scripts a season, as mandated by the Writers Guild of America. On a sitcom, there is a writers' room, and each script is outlined by committee, meaning that groups of people work together coming up with the basic story and structure. Then a writer (or writing team) goes on his own and hashes it out scene by scene, line by line. Then it's back to the writing room, where everyone works on polishing the scenes, adding situations and inserting one-liners, all duly recorded by the writing assistant who notes every word. The writers' room on a drama is not used as frequently. Usually the writer of the episode works independently from an outline generated by the writing team, then the executive producer does a rewrite for a final script.

DIRECTOR

Most shows, particularly dramas, use a stable of directors. TV directors can work on many different shows in the course of a season. This is less true in comedy, where directors like *Frasier*'s James Burrows tend to be part of the creative team, returning week after week to helm the show and give it a consistent tone. More likely, he or she is working freelance. More and more these days, executive producers are giving cast and crew members opportunities to direct, with more and more show stars also appearing in the "directed by" crawl. TV does not have *auteur* directors—the vision and tone of the show are created by the executive producer. The director is nonetheless in charge on the set. He or she must secure the best performances from the actors, re-create the feel of the show as envisioned by the executive producer, make sure the jokes work in a sitcom, coordinate all the below-the-line staff and bring the episode in on budget.

MUSIC BY

This credit goes to the individual who composes the music for the episode, creating original scores and compositions or adapting existing music and songs. The composer must match the tone and style of the music to the thematic and dramatic needs of the episode, while maintaining the overall tone and style of the show as crafted by the show's creator or executive producer. He or she therefore must understand the premise of the show and be familiar with its individual nuances. In many instances, the music of an episode can be as important to the drama or humor as a line of dialogue.

This is the composer of the show's theme. A signature of the show, the theme more than any single element captures the tone and feel of the drama or sitcom. The composer must understand the creator's concept, getting a feel for the actors, the dialogue, the style and pacing of the show before the show has even had a chance to air and evolve. It is a magical blend of intuition and art. As with everything in Hollywood, there is a Great Divide between film and TV—especially when it comes to composers. Few do both. Those in film see themselves in a tradition of classicists. The best theme makers of television, however, many times see their works transformed into part of pop culture itself, defining not only a show but many times an entire era.

Job Descriptions

EXECUTIVE CONSULTANT It's not uncommon for shows to have a consultant who serves as a hired-gun producer. This is usually a person with many years of television experience who can be called upon for help with story lines, cast, budgets, rewrites and network dealings. More often than not, this is a producer who once worked on the show full time and has been re-called to see that everything is kept creatively on track. In some cases, he is a special consultant in a particular field. On *ER*, these are medical personnel and MDs, who help suggest story lines and ensure a sense of reality about the show.

STORY EDITOR This is a lower-level staff writer—probably someone who's into their second season, having survived the ritual season-end head-rolling that follows the season finale. These writers work for the producers and head writers. They are not the bottom of the barrel, however. Staff writers, known as baby writers, are not always credited unless they have credit for actually writing a specific episode, in which case their credit goes above the line.

DIRECTOR OF PHOTOGRAPHY The corollary of a feature film's cinematographer, he or she is the head of the camera department and the camera operators, usually two or three behind the camera depending on the size of the show. When the director says, "I want to shoot this scene from here," it is the DP's job to make sure that is the shot the director gets—the angle, the lighting, the exposure. He matches the camera values and lighting from scene to scene. He also works closely with the first and second assistant loaders who load film and are responsible for film inventory.

CAMERA OPERATOR Responsible directly to the DP, the operator maintains the composition, focus and movement desired by the director of photography, ensures the quality of each shot, rejects any take that is deemed faulty, and is responsible for the proper functioning of his assigned camera.

PRODUCTION DESIGNER / ART DIRECTOR

The person designs the sets, figuring out how to turn a description of locale in a script into an actual location. He or she is responsible for researching and supervising all artwork associated with the production and assembling or constructing props, furniture and set decoration as well as backdrops and greenery. The designer also orders scale models made by a model builder and supervises the entire art department and budget.

EDITOR

Like his film counterpart, the editor works closely with the director in postproduction to cut all footage into a cohesive show, establishing pace, tone, style and capturing the director's vision.

Sometimes called the line producer, the production manager is the enforcer, dotting the i's and crossing the t's that the creative types do not have the time or stomach for. He is responsible for the money, ensuring that all departments come in on budget during the shoot. He is also responsible for adhering to all guild and union laws, from overtime and meals to safety issues.

The right and left hand of the director, the AD is responsible for just about everything. He or she is in charge of all traffic; all departments report to him or her. The keeper of the master list, the AD does all scheduling (including actors), making sure the crew does not rack up overtime. He makes sure lighting, costuming, hair, makeup and wardrobe is where, when and how the director wants it to be. It is the AD's voice that yells "Rolling!" at the beginning of a take and his that delivers the message "Cut!" over a walkie-talkie. But being at the nexus of all the action has its hazards: when the director or spoiled star trips, more often than not its the AD who takes the fall.

The second AD covers all the stuff the first AD has not gotten around to, which usually means generating all the daily shooting schedules for cast and crew, spending the first half of the day working on call sheets for the next day. He is also in charge of background in action scenes and deals directly with the extras. Most importantly, he should be able to do the first AD's job in case of illness or other industry ills—like firings.

ASSOCIATE PRODUCER

The associate producer helps the line producer much the way the second AD helps the first. There are a million details to tend to on a shoot, and the associate producer will see about 900,000 of them. It is often a title given to an assistant who's been promoted.

CASTING DIRECTOR He or she reports to the director and does the finding, interviewing, recommending and scheduling for the principal players, supporting cast and bit players. The casting director must not only keep abreast of emerging talent but have an eye for appraising on the spot the strengths and weaknesses of individuals and their suitability to play characters described in a script. It's a rare art: at its finest, it's almost magic.

COSTUME SUPERVISOR A critical job, especially in television, which is a pop force for setting style trends—think *Friends* and *Buffy the Vampire Slayer*— the costume supervisor determines the entire look of the characters, from Reebok to Roxy. In fact, the costume supervisor for *Buffy* recently signed on with a retailer to bring out a line of *Buffy* wear. The costume supervisor has to know everything, from current and breaking styles and labels, down to the body measurements and colorings of the actors. In the case of historical dramas and period pieces, the costumer works with the seamstress, cutters and fitters to create styles appropriate to the time.

A swap meet browser's dream job, this person works with the art director in dressing the set. Set dressing is anything not used as a prop, like a lamp, a phone book, a magazine. Think of all the junk piled around the *Friends'* apartment. Like the costumers, the set decorator must be aware not only of current trends and looks, but the styles of many eras and cultures. You wouldn't want Captain Picard's quarters looking like Dawson's bedroom.

A prop is anything that an actor picks up or uses in a scene; i.e., a telephone, a gun, a camera. The prop master is in charge of reading the script to find what props will be needed in each scene, then scouring the studio and prop houses to make sure they are on the set the day scheduled. That can take a lot of ingenuity, depending upon whether the script calls for just a simple cell phone or a Borg transmitter.

He or she is in charge of makeup for all actors and determines the look for each character. The key makeup artist "designs" the facial look, at the same time ensuring that the actors are balanced photogenically (i.e., no shiny noses). Versed in all state laws governing cosmetology, the makeup artist is in charge of this "street" makeup, as well as character makeup (including latex and prosthetics), special-effects makeup (using latex, tubes, plastics and liquids to create the illusion of, say, an open wound) and body makeup.

KEY HAIRSTYLIST

This person determines the appropriate hairstyles for all characters in all scenes, working with the key makeup artists and overseeing the assistant hairdressers. Like music and costuming, a hairstylist can help create the style and spin of a show, especially youth-oriented programs that create pop trends. *Friends*' Jennifer Aniston's hairstyle became a standard cut at salons across the country.

This person is in charge of the sound department and is responsible for anything that can be heard, from dialogue to background noise to special sound effects. He or she works closely with the director and director of photography during the shot to optimize sound quality, overseeing the boom operator (the second-in-command sound person who actually carries the boom) and the utility sound person (the third-in-command who pulls the cables) and ensures the proper placement of microphones, booms, fishing poles and makes sure there is no extraneous noise.

This is the person responsible for getting all cast and crew from one set to another and to outside locations, and coordinating equipment trucks and cast trailers.

CRAFT SERVICES

This is the person responsible for catering the shoots and the most popular individual on the set.

POSTPRODUCTION SUPERVISOR

The postproduction supervisor not only schedules all editing and ADR (sound and looping) after principal photography is wrapped, he or she is also the liaison to the network or studio, calming jittery execs when necessary and often working with them on promo reels for the show.

GAFFER The head electrician, he or she oversees all lighting needs, working closely with the DP to create the right tone of each scene. The gaffer supplies all the lighting mechanics: luminaries, gloves, stands, mounting devices, connectors, power sources, scrims, diffusion gels and the like. He oversees the lighting crew, including the best boys (lighting technicians), riggers and special operators.

KEY GRIP The Bekins man of the TV industry, the grip is in charge of moving any equipment that does not have a plug on it, like foils and dollies, and for safely preparing the set. He works closely with the DP to expedite the lighting, camera placement and camera movement procedures.

SCRIPT SUPERVISOR This person has the daunting task of making sure the entire script is covered correctly and that every scene is shot from the right angle. He or she also has the thankless job of watching for continuity—making sure that if an actor has a certain color of nail polish one day, the actor has the same color for the same scene the next, knowing all along that any slipups will be immortalized in the next Hollywood trivia book.

BEST BOY There is no one best boy. The term means second in command. Thus, there is a best boy gaffer and a best boy grip. The positions usually involve doing the paperwork, keeping time cards, overseeing the equipment and waiting for a promotion.

music

For good reason, record and film companies have been crossing over into each other's turfs for years. Geffen Records and then-Dutch-owned Polygram Records were just two of the record giants to create filmed-entertainment divisions back in the '80s and '90s. Until its sale to Seagram in 1999, Dutch-owned

Polygram Records and Britain's EMI were the largest record companies in the world. And, of course, most of the major studios, including Warner Bros., Universal and Columbia (later Sony) all ran huge large music divisions with scores of labels.

In many ways, the recording business probably has more in common with the studio system than any other entertainment industry. Like Hollywood, the record industry was dominated for years by a handful of recording companies such as Columbia and RCA Victor, which routinely bound their artists to exclusive long-term contracts. Like the stars of filmdom, the recording business was dominated by small coterie of marquee names. In the early days, the most commercial artists came from big bands like those led by Harry James, Glenn Miller and Count Basie—their front men and star vocals. There was the occasional crossover jazz great, the torch singers and the perennial big sellers, Broadway show tunes and light opera. But though Hollywood had A and B movies, for the most part it remained a homogenous business. Some stars were bigger than others; some pictures were more important than others. But all were products of the same studios. By contrast, the recording industry was more or less ghettoized, populated by a dog-eat-dog world of small labels and independents which specialized in the various genres—blues, R&B, country-western, gospel, jazz, classical, opera. The major record companies operated their own subdivisions and labels to compete in each market. Each musical genre inhabited its own world, with its own artists, its own producers, its own labels, even its own talent managers who tended to handle one style of artist.

The business began to change, however, with the arrival of its first pop superstar, Frank Sinatra, in the '40s. His records sold in the millions and dominated the radio waves, creating a cultural whirlpool that sucked in a new and untapped market of postwar teens and young adults with money to spend on 45s. If Sinatra had tapped the market, Elvis Presley in the '50s exploited it, at the same time creating the notion of the rock star as cultural icon. The cult of personality that began dominating the record charts spread to entire groups, with the coming of the Beatles and the Rolling Stones and other supergroups of the '60s.

The revolution in recording technology, the rise of CDs and music videos, the "alternative rock" stars, the evolution of entire musical genres that were as much cultural as musical, all fed a celebrity-based market in the following decades, transforming the entire business. Labels no longer looked so much for a certain sound, say, like record producer Phil Spector's famous "Wall of Sound." Popular in the first half of the 1960s, Spector would assemble black female singers into various vocal groups, usually fronted in the studio by his wife, Darlene Love, then back them with his signature sound: a rich, driving orchestral wave. But increasingly, labels looked for breakout bands with distinctive styles and directions or for a genre like reggae or Seattle grunge that captured not only a sound but a culture: And in the past few decades, the recording business has exploded globally, with international movements like the punk-inspired British new wave, Euro techno-pop, world music and Latin-based Tejano rock.

■ ■ ■

At the center of all the action are the talent managers and the attorneys. In the music business, talent agents are pretty much limited to signing commercial and film deals for big-name recording artists or, perhaps, even helping with tours. MCA, the Music Company of America, began as a booking agency for big bands and musical acts back in the days when club engagements paid the bills, not recording deals. Anyone who saw actor Tom Hanks's small-budget movie *That Thing You Do!* knows that behind any successful artist or band lies the talent manager. It is the manager who finds the willing label and, along with the entertainment attorney, negotiates the artist's recording deals. But unlike agents, the manager is very involved in crafting the artist's direction and sound, helping his client not only to hone his or her art but also find a voice and an audience, a niche in the marketplace. The manager typically has input in selecting the producer who will create the artist's album in the studio and may even suggest studio musicians, engineers and even cover art. The manager also consults on club bookings and tours, having input even on what acts or artists should be on the same bill as his client.

Unlike film or television, the recording business is not project-driven. The artist and his or her talent is the commodity being sold, not a concept or a story idea to which producers attach talent as they go. Generally, a recording artist or band is signed to a one-album deal, with the record company retaining the option to do one or two other albums. In a typical deal, the artist receives an advance against future royalties, what is called a "recording fund." A typical fund for a "baby band," or an unestablished group, varies between $150,000 to $500,000. The record company considers much of this advance recoupable. The artist, for instance, is responsible for the production costs of the album, including the producers, the studio rental and the salaries of the engineers and studio musicians. If the label pays for special promotions or outside marketing people, typically it considers 50 percent of that outlay recoupable. Many times the label will pay for tour support, then deduct 50 percent of those expenditures from royalties. Similarly, the cost of producing videos is generally considered recoupable. What exactly is or isn't recoupable depends upon the individual contract and the stature of the artist. Labels anxious to sign—or keep—big-name artists will many times waive numerous recoupable expenses they are likely to charge less established artists.

In general, new artists do not see a lot of royalties at the beginning. And despite the well-known grumblings of many bands who feel their advances were eagerly eaten up by the insatiable maw of record company overhead, the fact is even first-time artists can see royalties—though it may take a while. It took Sheryl Crow a year or two to see royalties from the sales of her first album, *Tuesday Night Music Club*, but she saw them.

Despite the continuing shift of money and power to the artists themselves, the record companies, like the studios, control the industry. The artist depends on the label for producing, marketing and distributing his or her music. Though the artist, in effect, can go off on his own to produce his album, rejecting any and all input from the label, ultimately the label has the power to release or not release the recording, effectively negating months, or even years, of blood, sweat and tears. Unlike Hollywood, there is no "turnaround" in the recording industry; that is, recording companies do not allow rival companies to buy up the rights to an album by reimbursing them for production expenses. It is this powerful stick they wield which keeps young up-and-coming artists under a label's thumb.

The gatekeeper to a label is the A&R department, which stands for "artists and repertoire." These are the talent scouts for the label. A&R reps get access to new material through two primary routes: (1) listening to recorded material that has been submitted to them from managers, publishers and attorneys representing bands (for liability reasons, most labels don't allow unsolicited material, much like movie studios' policies about scripts); or (2) by going out to live performances at clubs and other venues to scout talent. A&R people tend to be young, attuned to current trends and have a good ear for a commercial sound. They are also incredible networkers, constantly in motion, talking to people in the business—other managers, band members, club owners, booking agents, critics—always trying to get a lead on a hot new artist or group.

When A&R people do locate an artist or band that looks promising, they present their "finds" at meetings with the label president and the heads of the various departments. Here, they will play any recordings, or "cuts," the singer or group has already done. The executives then give a thumbs-up or thumbs-down to signing the act. If the company is interested, the artist's attorney and manager work out a deal with label's representatives, usually legal affairs, the A&R rep and, when necessary, the input of the label president.

Once an artist or group has been signed, the A&R rep works closely with him or her to produce the album, function as a creative liaison between the label and the artist. This entails selecting a producer, choosing the types of songs to record, honing a particular sound and so on. If a band is young and relatively new, it probably will not have much of a repertoire and may need help fine-tuning an individual sound and style. The rep and producer, both knowledgeable about what is commercial, can make suggestions, helping define the sound of the band. Once the album has been recorded, it is played for the label's department heads and key players, who make comments much the way a producer and director will give a screenwriter feedback on a script. Opinions might range from acceptance of the album to a request for minor changes (cut the length of the songs, drop certain songs, add others) to outright rejection of the album, at which time the band will go back into the studio to try again.

For obvious reasons, this is often where art and commerce collide. Musicians have a vision of how they want the album to sound. The label heads, however, are concerned with commercial viability and, since they're fronting the costs, they have the right to ask for changes they deem necessary. Some contracts give control to the artist; most contracts give control to the label. In all cases, the two parties try to work out differences and find compromises. But in the end, it is the label that has the right to accept or reject the album.

Once the album is accepted, the various other departments at the label kick into gear. The band is assigned to the product management department, which is responsible for the coordination of all departments. Just as a product manager at General Mills might be responsible for Cheerios, a product manager at a label may be responsible for the Backstreet Boys, making sure all the departments are coordinated and working together and on schedule to get the product out to the public and market it thoroughly.

Production handles the actual physical manufacturing of the CD, tape or vinyl disc (yes, they still make them). Working with the various departments, a "guesstimate" is made as to how many units to produce. A familiar term is "gold" or "platinum." SoundScan awards a gold

Touring: The Long and Winding Road

Record labels do not have a "tour" department, per se, but performing is an integral part of the industry, helping to both establish artists and promote album sales. Various departments are involved in this, from A&R to product management to publicity. The band's manager and road manager handle most of the actual nuts-and-bolts details of a tour, with the other departments lending support. When you get into the level of, say, the Rolling Stones, the entire label gets involved, but much of it is also handled by outside tour support companies.

While every band's deal is unique, the label will often defray certain costs of touring that are considered a recoupable expense. The band also gets a daily stipend to pay for living expenses during the tour. In the end, the artist and the tour promoter share in the profits from ticket sales.

The big, established artists and bands usually can make the decision of when and where to tour, usually hitting only the biggest venues and traveling first class all the way. For newcomers, it's "produce, or move on," much the same as what goes on at the movie studios. Once again, art meets commerce. The collision isn't always pretty, but it works. ▶

album when 500,000 units sell, platinum when it hits 1,000,000. Often, to generate publicity, an album will be reported to have "shipped" platinum, which means the label has produced and shipped to retailers a million units in anticipation of equivalent sales. However, for an album to be certified gold or platinum, it needs to sell that number of units. If it tanks, retailers have the right to return the disc to the label for a refund.

While the album is being produced, the art department works with the musicians, producer and manager to come up with a concept for the album packaging. Photos are shot, artwork is ordered and created, liner notes are produced. The cover is a crucial component of marketing the band, since the look and feel of the artwork, much like a band's costuming, helps define not only the sound of the band but the audience the label hopes to market to.

One of the most important departments is promotions, which is responsible for shopping the singles to radio. Promotions people listen to the finished album and select which song(s) they think have the best chance to become hit singles. Again, they and the artists might be at odds over this, but the promotions people often have the last word (though an established act might have more say in which songs will be selected). The promotions people send out tapes/CDs to the radio programmers, meet with them personally to play the songs, or invite them to "listening parties." This is a crucial part of the process in that so much of the music industry is radio driven. If a song doesn't get airplay, the album will have a very difficult time getting exposure and, thus, sales. In years past, this has been a controversial area. Charges of "payola" have been investigated many times, with critics charging that radio programmers and managers are often courted with lavish gifts, promo goodies, concert tickets junkets and even cash and drugs.

While the promotions department works the radio stations, the sales department targets retail chains like Tower Records as well as smaller stores to place orders. The sales department sends buyers quarterly "books," or catalogs, that detail what they have coming up, including descriptions of the acts, the people involved with the project, the sound, etc. If available, they'll send along recorded samples.

Advertising/merchandising supports the sales staff by creating ads for print, television and other media, working with the art department and purchasing space for those ads. They also create point-of-purchase displays that you see in retail stores (these are paid for by the label, not the retailer) as well as buy space in "listening stations," those areas in most retail stores nowadays where customers can listen to selected albums.

Once an album is nearing completion, publicity works to get press on the album/artist. If it's an unknown baby band, they would pitch it to various media outlets, trying to get reviews of the album and stories/interviews on the band itself. They would coordinate interviews, photo shoots and press events (which include meet-and-greet dinners between artists and journalists, listening parties, getting writers out to shows, junkets to an out-of-town show, etc.).

Of course if it's an established band, the press usually comes to the publicity department clamoring for time with the artist. Some bands, especially very successful acts like

U2 or the Rolling Stones, might hire outside independent PR firms to handle their publicity. Of course, at this point, it becomes more about deflecting publicity and doling out the artist's time among all the various media outlets that want to cover them. ∎

Job Descriptions

above the line

COMPOSER / LYRICIST

As in the film industry, assigning credit to a particular project can be a pretty tricky business. For one thing, just as a film credit does not delineate who wrote the initial screenplay, who was brought in to do a character rewrite or who did the dialogue polish, so, too, albums do not necessarily distinguish between who composed the music and who wrote the lyrics. In the case of collaborators like Bernie Taupin and Elton John, everyone knows who composed the music and who thought up the lyrics. But often times, both music and lyrics can be a collaborative effort. In the case of Madonna's "Drowned World/Substitute for Love," there are five writers credited: Madonna, William Orbit, Rod McKuen, Anita Kerr and David Collins. In addition, there is "sampling" (the practice of incorporating snippets of other songs into new compositions, sometimes legally with credits, sometimes not). This is the case with "Why I Follow the Tigers," a song originally written and recorded by McKuen and Kerr and performed by the San Sebastian Strings. For songs that were not sampled, Madonna, like many musicians, probably handled most of the lyrics and the others the music, with some degree of overlap. It's not uncommon for artists to sit down face-to-face and work on songs before or during the recording process, but it's just as likely the two creations were done separately, even by fax.

Entangling things further, the writing credit at times is not so much a professional acknowledgement as a legal nicety. On the Rolling Stones' *Bridges to Babylon* album, k.d. lang and writing partner Ben Mink landed a writing credit on "Anybody Seen My Baby?" Most likely, since the song was similar to lang and Mink's hit "Constant Craving," discussions between the Stones' camp and lang's took place, an acceptable remuneration was agreed to, and the credit approved.

The publisher ultimately oversees the copyright usage of the song or musical composition. In many cases, a publisher like Warner/Chappell Music, Inc. may be the copyright owner because the writer has sold them ownership outright. In some cases, the publisher may share partial ownership with the writer. In other cases, the publisher may simply act as an administrator of the copyright, collecting royalties for the writer. The publisher issues licenses to ad agencies for commercial use, to filmmakers and to other artists, collects royalties and promotes the song and the writer. The publisher also exploits the work in five categories: merchandising royalties; synchronization rights for movies, TV and commercials; performance rights; print royalties and dramatic use rights for stage. In the case of *Ray of Light*, both WB Music Corp. and Webo Girl Publishing, Inc., Madonna's publishing company, share the copyright. It's not uncommon for individual songs to have yet additional publisher credits. On *Ray of Light*, No Tomato Music, Future Furniture Music and Chrysalis Music Limited are also credited; these are usually the publishing companies of the credited co-writers. Depending upon the number of writers involved, publishing credits can become a labyrinth of large and small companies and administrators.

PRODUCER

In many ways, the producer is like the feature-film director. Most are either engineers, technical wizards, "knob turners" who intimately involve themselves in the nuts and bolts of the recording process, or musicians, content to let the engineer handle the technical aspects. In either event, the producer is responsible for the project in general, for eliciting the best performance possible from the artist, for working on song arrangements (determining whether a song should be slower, faster, what type of instrumentation and overall sound or ambiance it should have, whether a particular refrain should be repeated or deleted, etc.) A producer is also cheerleader and psychiatrist. If Madonna's going to record a slow, mellow ballad, for example, the producer might make sure the studio is cleared of all extraneous personnel to create intimacy. He might know that Madonna does this type of song best in the morning or late in the evening and would schedule the session accordingly. On the other hand, if it's a raucous feeling they're after, the producer might try to create that ambiance by bringing in some friends or guest musicians. On the Mavericks' country band 1998 album, *Trampoline*, much of the recording was done in a huge former church to help create a loose, party feeling on the album. They had an open-door policy for musician friends and family members to drop by; on some occasions, they literally had a fiesta going on, with margaritas flowing to help set the mood. It would be the producer's job to create and control these settings.

Producer credits can vary wildly on an album, from the artist himself to a single producer for the entire project to various combinations thereof. In the case of *Ray of Light*, each song has a separate producer credit, Madonna being one of the producers on every cut. The other producer on most of the other cuts is Orbit. Credited producers on particular songs include Marius De Vries and Patrick Leonard. The reasons for this are many, but all grow out of the unique and complex role of the producer. Generally speaking, the artist is responsible for the overall conception of the album and individual songs; he/she/they decide with whom they want to work as producer. (In certain cases, however, the producer is responsible for the overall concept and sound. Babyface, for instance, simply fits an artist into his own concept.)

Madonna chose William Orbit as her main producer (he also gets songwriting credits, so he had quite a bit to do with the creative process), but she added additional producers (De Vries and Leonard) on songs where she was looking for a particular sound. Unlike a film or TV show, an album is really an anthology or works packaged together—sometimes by widely varying talents.

Job Descriptions

ENGINEER The engineer is the person who literally sits behind the control panel in the booth outside the studio to record the songs. If it's the artist and producer's job to conceptualize the sound they want to achieve, it's the engineer's job to make it happen and capture it in the recording. The engineer is the knob-turner, the person who sets recording levels, determines sound quality (i.e., reverb, bass, treble, distortion), rolls tape or DAT equipment and punches buttons to cut certain sounds in or out of the recording at given times. He might work with any number of assistants, whose job it is to set microphones and run cable from them into the mixing board, handle tape reels or DAT machines, set up sound baffles, take care of technical aspects of instruments, even run for food and drinks. Generally speaking, the producer chooses the engineer he/she wants to work with. In the case of *Ray of Light*, several engineers are credited, none with specific songs, but each with a specialty, from jazz to blues/rock to rap. Songs may be recorded "live" in their entirety or pieced together in separate tracks (i.e., guitar, drums, vocals, strings, etc. can be recorded separately at different times on individual tracks and then ultimately mixed together). Depending upon the complexity of the song, it might contain 4, 8,

16, up to 64 or more tracks of individual instruments or "overdubs" (a vocal or guitar solo might be recorded or rerecorded on separate tracks to add fullness to the sound). It's the engineer's job to manage that process.

STUDIO The studio is the actual location where the artists and crew convene to perform and record the album. Sometimes albums are recorded during live performances in a club or other venue. Sometimes individual songs might be recorded in different studios in different parts of the world in order to capture a particular sound a studio is noted for or to accommodate the musician's availability. In this case, *Ray of Light* was recorded at a single studio, Larrabee Studios North in Universal City, California.

MIXER

Usually during the recording process, the producer and engineer have already made a rough mix that approximates what they're seeking. In fact, the producer may be an engineer, but he will bring in another engineer to be the mixer. The sound mixer combines, or "mixes," the individual tracks into a single version. That means volumes of individual instruments are decided. If a heavy drum-and-bass dance sound is desired, the mixer gives those instruments prominence, while pulling others back. For a ballad, piano and vocals might be given prominence. Strings might be brought up for certain sections and brought down for others. It's a crucial part of the process—especially on dance and techno albums—and the mixer can completely change the final outcome of a song. It's so crucial, in fact, that mixers like Bob Clearmountain have become nearly legendary. Often these days, remixes are done of songs that don't appear on the original album. A mixer will come in and remix a song to give it a completely different sound, often releasing it as single for radio or as a dance mix.

MASTERER   Mastering is the final production phase in which the final mixed version of all the songs are put down onto a final "master" version from which all the mass-produced dubs (albums, CDs, tapes) will be copied. In the old days of lacquer albums, the masterer quite literally determined how deep to cut the grooves in the record. In this digital day and age, much of this is no longer pertinent. Essentially, the masterer determines final volume levels of songs and, at the artist and producer's discretion, places the songs in the correct order in which they'll appear on the final product.

MUSICIANS   In a typical band project, individual members and the instruments they play are clearly listed, including studio musicians who normally work for scale. The artist or band members who are cutting the album are obviously above-the-line, not only sharing in royalties but usually working under contract to a particular record company. Those deals are cut individually and can be every bit as complicated as a film deal, though probably not as imaginative. On *Ray of Light*, certain cuts are credited to a few specific individuals. Fergus Gerrand, for example, gets a drums credit on "Drowned World/Substitute for Love" and "Swim" and a percussion credit on "Mer Girl." Pablo Cook gets a flute credit on "Swim," and Marc Moreau, who works with Rod Stewart, gets a guitar credit on "Skin."

CONDUCTOR

The conductor is usually the arranger hired by the artist or the producer. All three will then hire the necessary musicians for session work. All have their favorites. Other musicians typically are found in the philharmonic of the city in which the recording is taking place. In the case of *Ray of Light*, Susie Katayama, a violinist, cellist and producer, used the Los Angeles Philharmonic union members. They are paid union scale and are often accompanied to the session by a union rep, who makes sure musicians are treated and paid accordingly. The producer will work with the conductor to indicate what type of sound is desired, and, of course, it's the conductor's job to elicit that performance from the orchestra.

ARRANGER

An arranger is a musician or composer who writes out the string arrangements before the players are brought in to record the tracks. Arrangers may be brought in for other musical pieces as well, such as percussion or wind, depending on the sophistication, scope—and budget —of the album.

TECHNICIANS These individuals are subspecialists: guitar technicians or drum techs. They are somewhat akin to roadies, the support members who load, unload and set up a band's sound equipment—amps, guitars, keyboards, mixers, etc.—during live concert performances. But studio techs are more highly trained, used by artists to maintain and monitor their instruments, making sure, for instance, that guitars are tuned, replacing broken strings and seeing to faulty pickups and amps.

SPECIAL THANKS TO Albums are often laden with a "Special Thanks" section in which the artist acknowledges people who have in some way or another contributed to or helped with the album. Unlike the legalese of publishing credits, this section is often very loose, freewheeling, touchy-feely and heartfelt, the music industry's version of the Academy Award acceptance speech. On *Ray of Light*, Madonna even managed to give special thanks for creative and spiritual guidance.

MANAGERS

While managers sometimes seem a luxury for actors who already have agents, managers are a necessity for musical artists. For up-and-coming artists, the manager is the road to recognition, seeking out labels, making sure record company executives see the acts, working with the A&R rep, advising contract negotiations, even securing airtime for their clients. The manager also works closely with publicists in determining the amount of press the artist will do, consults about bookings on the TV talk show circuit and interfaces with road managers during a tour.

The album cover art has become almost as notorious as what's inside. Depending upon the artist, the photographer may have little or a lot of control. In Madonna's case, she had a great deal of input on how the shoot went, though clearly with photographer Mario Testino's credits (he has shot everyone from Elton John and Janet Jackson to Princess Di), she chose him for his reputation and instinct, not his ability to take orders.

ART DIRECTOR / DESIGNER

The art director and designer are responsible for coming up with the overall look and concept of the album or CD packaging, including photos, typography, illustrations, logos, etc. In the case of *Ray of Light*, the concept is very simple: portraits of a windblown Madonna against a silvery-blue background done by Kevin Reagan, whose credits include Guns N' Roses, Rickie Lee Jones, Neil Young and Alanis Morissette.

PUBLICIST

Publicists coordinate all press requests, interviews, photo shoots, etc. They help their clients clarify what they want—and don't want—to reveal to the media. They know who are sympathetic critics and journalists and who might give their client a hard time, in which case ground rules are usually set before an interview is granted—or denied altogether. Their job is to ensure that the album-buying public sees only the positive image their client and the record company wants seen. Some artists use the in-house publicity team of the record label, others hire independents. Madonna uses Liz Rosenberg, an in-house publicist at Warner Records who specializes in handling the label's big guns, like Madonna, Chrissie Hynde of the Pretenders and others.

new media

I t's not hard visualizing a roomful of junior executives sitting around a few years from now chuckling at the term "new media." Jack Warner probably had a similar guffaw thinking about talkies in 1930 or CBS mogul William Paley about that magical invisible signal called a "television broadcast" by

1955. Truth is, before the toddling two-digit millennium has even shed its Pampers, "new media" will be the only media. If anything, the term will be much more useful delineating the social and financial gulf between "new media" billionaire CEOs and a fading club of "old media" multimillionaires.

Though the term is a catchall for a host of ongoing technological breakthroughs—in hardware, software and systems, if not in pure science and engineering—most frequently it is associated with things around or near the Internet. Its genesis is as foggy as its definition. Al Gore's claims to the contrary, the Internet was, if not born then at least conceived, over the Labor Day weekend of 1969 in the School of Engineering and Applied Sciences at the University of California, Los Angeles. Known as the ARPANET, the first node of what would grow to become the worldwide Net was funded by the Pentagon's Advanced Research Projects Agency, or ARPA. Spawned in response to the Soviet Union's launch of the satellite Sputnik in 1958, ARPA was founded to promote scientific research, especially research and development work in computer science, through the nation's universities and research centers. Each researcher was given a computer by ARPA. The ARPANET grew out of an attempt to link all the agency researchers' computers to one system in order to share information. UCLA constructed the first of 10 nodes, which it tested over that Labor Day weekend more than 30 years ago. Eventually, the nascent 10 nodes expanded to connect the entire country, becoming the rudimentary architecture of what would become the Internet.

For decades, the Internet remained pretty much a research-archive service, an information highway, whereby government agencies, academic institutions and research facilities could share information. By 1970, the Net was used to control a satellite hovering above the United States by sending messages from the East Coast to the West Coast. The founders never saw a need for more than 64 computers. But by the late 1980s, the number of computers logging onto the Internet had soared into the millions. E-mail became a standard medium of instant communication for both personal computer users and for large corporations. At the same time, smaller institutions, special interest and advocacy groups, and private individuals discovered the Internet was a cheap, efficient and incredibly effective way to get out information to a huge population. Government agencies, universities, libraries, archival services, even small businesses began dispersing information via Web sites. Web sites, or Web pages, were basically data sites, each with its own address, where users could stop, browse and download information. Many had click-on addresses which could take the user instantaneously to related data sites. These millions of data sites evolved into the World Wide Web. Though intimately interconnected, the Internet and the World Wide Web are not the same thing. The term "superinformation highway" became a media cliché for the data procuring and sharing abilities of the Internet, but it was nonetheless a fairly accurate metaphor. The Internet is very much like a giant infrastructure, linked by millions of machines, connecting hundred of thousands of electronic highways, streets and roads. If the Internet is like a huge network of highways and roads that allows the computer user to navigate to the smallest back alleys, then the World Wide Web can be seen as the equivalent of all the billboards along those highways, the information sites where travelers can attain information. To extend the analogy, the more sophisticated and intricately designed Web sites are more like roadside hotels, where travelers can stop and stay for awhile.

By the '90s, there were some 50 million computers with access to what had become the World Wide Web. But still, despite the grandiose predictions by seers and industry wildcatters, the Web seemed a playground mostly for gearheads, conspiracy nuts and librarians with time on their hands.

All that changed radically with the explosion of personal computer use, the rise of Internet service providers such as America Online, @Home Network, AT&T and Earthlink, to name a few. These ISPs provided organized Internet access, allowing users to find quickly and easily the sort of information they were looking for as well as offering a means of discovering new data sources. Meanwhile, search engines like Yahoo!, Excite and AltaVista expanded the capabilities of the ISP hardware, creating Web servers with the latest in digital design software to attract particular audiences, sculpting imaginative new interactive sites and linking Web sites of similar interests and functions. Together, the ISPs and search engines transformed the Internet from an esoteric, seemingly endless digital database to a hip, colorful new world of virtual fun for Web surfing and discovering thousands of new portals which sprung, Minervalike, fully formed into this new marketplace. Even better, ISPs provided Web machines that allowed the service's users to create their own Web sites. There were game rooms, porn rooms, social chat rooms, movie guides, gossip sites, news sites, Libertarian sites. Fearing to be left behind, major corporations set up Web sites if only to maintain a presence in the marketplace. They were for fun, for image, for education, for communication—for everything except profit.

Capitalism logged on to the Internet with the coming of e-commerce pioneers, which created Web sites to sell goods directly to the PC consumer, cutting out not only the middleman but even the hassle of driving to the local mall. Soon, businesses such as book retailer Amazon.com, Ticketmaster, and eToys, not to mention travel agencies, online securities trading firms and virtual auction houses were selling goods over the worldwide mall. But though Web sites were gussied up with bells and whistles like click-on chat rooms, book reviews and Top 10 users' lists, these were really just virtual window dressings to bring in browsers off the digital sidewalk. Entertaining, they were not entertainment.

In fact, the entertainment industry appeared slow to cash in on the Web. The studios, networks and record companies, like most U.S. companies, were quick to create corporate Web sites for PR and marketing purposes, but there were no programs, no shows, no films looking for a virtual box-office gross.

The void of such traditional artistic entertainment media as film, video and music on the Internet had as much to do with a lag in technology as a lack of creative ideas. For one thing, old-fashioned phone lines and coaxial cable, which served as conduits for most of the population's link to the Internet, were relatively slow. And they would not be able to handle the high-quality visuals and sound effects of online games and movies that were being talked about in the future. Cable servers, whose fiber-optic cables could carry state-of-the-art digital images and sound both to PCs and the family tube, began gearing up to take over the marketplace.

Studios, search engines and content creators began looking for "strategic alliances," the result being a round of merger mania between entertainment conglomerates, cable companies and new media suppliers. Paramount, purchased by Sumner Redstone's cable and television giant Viacom after a much publicized takeover fight with entertainment icon Barry Diller, had already positioned itself in the cable marketplace, but had done little with its cable arm other than using its Web sites as promotional vehicles for MTV, Nickelodeon, VH1 and studio feature releases. In 1999, however, the corporation, under the lead of MTV Networks, began aggressively pursuing online ventures, forging an alliance with John Malone's cable and Internet powerbroker Liberty Media to create an interactive music TV channel and with AT&T, which also owns high-speed Internet provider Excite@Home. In 1997, AT&T began its purchase of the other cable giant, Telecommunications Inc., or TCI, and purchased high-speed Internet pioneer @Home. Time Warner, which began upgrading its extensive cable services into digital, has positioned itself to become a major new media player, launching Warner Bros. Online and the multimillion dollar mega-Web site, Entertaindom, one of the industry's biggest Internet projects. The Walt Disney Company, too, has moved to become a major player in the next millennium, buying 43 percent of Infoseek and folding the provider into its new Internet portal Go Network to compete with search engines like Yahoo!. An indication of just how important the studio sees the Internet in its future business portfolio became clear in September 1999 when it appointed one of its hottest and most respected television executives to overhaul its entire new media division. Even Diller's USA Network moved to acquire search engine Lycos in 1999, giving the independent cable network mogul a foothold on the Internet. Meanwhile, Sony Corp. launched two online units, Columbia TriStar Interactive and game-oriented Sony Online.

Despite the temblors in the entertainment and financial media, the net effect of the new-media merger mania was mostly confined to creating a whole new club of young, semi-iconoclastic, wholly hip and often obnoxiously confident multimillionaire CEOs who benefitted from the mergers and IPOs. In Hollywood, new media served essentially as a crossover medium for new projects or as a promotional tool, an "add-on" as executives would term it, to the industry's traditional fare: feature films, television shows and record albums.

The first signs that new media had cracked the Hollywood power lunch were a rash of CD-ROM-inspired feature films such as Disney's *Super Mario Bros.*, Sony's *Street Fighter* and New Line's *Mortal Kombat*. But other than taking the title characters and a perceived ready-made audience, the films had virtually nothing to do with the virtual world that inspired them. Worse, most were box-office disappointments.

The Internet was used almost exclusively as a promotional tool. None of the new Web sites took advantage of the

Internet's one truly unique quality: its interactive potential. Even more fatal when it came to attracting young Web surfers, the sites were definitely not hip, offering information about shows in another medium and remaining devoid of original content. Users logging on to Columbia TriStar's site for its teen drama *Dawson's Creek*, for instance, could access a "private" interactive journal of one of the characters, which amounted to little more than episode summaries. A page tied to the daytime soap *Days of Our Lives* allowed users to chat about the characters. At News Corp.'s site for *The X-Files*, Web surfers could read plot summaries of past episodes or join chat rooms to rap about the show.

The effects of the mergers—the fusion of Web site creators, corporate capital and Hollywood know-how—began to surface in the final years of the decade. One of the early precursors came from NBC. Having observed that its hour-long drama *Homicide: Life on the Street* had garnered a strong following in its chat rooms, the network began an Internet version of the show called *Homicide: Second Shift*, hiring actors and staging new episodes online. In 1999, the network had worked an online story line about a ritual murder into the prime-time drama, at the same time creating an interactive Web site where online viewers could examine evidence or, say, look through a detective's notebook.

The summer of '99's surprise hit, the independently released *The Blair Witch Project*, was dubbed the first Internet movie, because of its unprecedented and imaginative use of the Internet in its marketing campaign. Crippled by comparison to the multimillion-dollar marketing budgets of the major studios, the *Blair Witch* distributors decided to open the horror film in limited release, accompanied by a modest TV and print ad campaign. In the meantime, to build word-of-mouth buzz, a crucial component in capturing the youth film market, the distributors created a *Blair Witch* Web site, which purportedly carried some of the last surviving film footage and diary entries written by one of the perished filmmakers. The Web site attracted millions of hits, both hyping interest in the movie and adding to the marketing myth that the events in the film really happened. By the time the movie had been expanded to wide general release, the youth audience was primed to make it one of the summer's blockbuster hits.

Magazines, too, were among the first to translate traditional print medium to the Internet. Browsers witnessed the emergence of virtual magazines like the E! channel's *E! Online*, *Salon* and *Slate*, which were designed like old-style magazines with feature stories, columns, reviews and photographs, but sported one big difference: electronic magazines could be updated hourly and offered digital, interactive add-ons like chat rooms and video clips that their flat, paperbound cousins could never hope to replicate. Behind the high-tech designs, however, lies a very old-fashioned idea: advertising dollars.

The challenge, in fact, was to find a way to generate profit through entertainment online. Most experts agreed that to accomplish this entertainment companies would have to provide Internet users something that did not mimic TV and film, where the product was dictated to the audience. Besides the ability to call up—and even download—films from limitless archives and "virtually" attend music concerts by logging on to live Webcasts (all service-oriented businesses), the industry has begun to think in terms of original, interactive programming, allowing users to follow different plot lines or even make up their own, controlling what the title characters do.

Warner Bros. Entertaindom represents one of the most ambitious projects. Divided into four areas, the megasite includes Playdom, offering online games and interactive crafts projects with other users, Toondom, presenting children's programming as well as original cartoons, Screendom, showing television, movies and live Webcasts of movie openings, and Rhythmdom, featuring online music and live concert Webcasts. Disney has been overhauling its Blast Web site, adding collaborative games like a treasure hunt which allows up to 24 players to communicate and play at the same time. The industry hopes to make money off these sites by selling advertising, taking slices of the electronic transactions, selling pay-per-view events and, ultimately, subscriptions, much the same way cable TV charges.

Music may be the biggest player in new media, accounting soon for 28 percent of all Internet transactions. Next on the market will be a new generation of machines which are part computer, part television and part conduit to the Net and will function as digital jukeboxes, allowing users to pluck songs or albums from the Internet for personal compilations. These playlists could then be transferred to a credit card-sized "flash card" to carry with you and play an a small CD-type player.

Instead of buying music on a CD or even a digital file, fans can "rent" music for a monthly fee, drawing from a limitless cyber-archive of songs which can be "streamed" to them like a personalized radio playlist. Every Pearl Jam or

Rolling Stones concert could be instantly available on the Internet. Or fans streaming from a concert could stop by the lobby kiosk and buy a flash card of the just-finished concert, then return home and call up an e-mail from the band commenting on the night's performance.

Like all new media, the Grand Canyon leap in cyber-recording has accompanied a new breakthrough in technology: an audio file format called MP3, originally created by a German research facility to compress CD-quality audio files to one-tenth their size. Joined by other new computer audio players like Liquid Audio, Windows Media Player and a2b Music, MP3 players allow students on campuses across the country to illegally download pirated songs on the Internet, causing a whole new headache for the recording industry, which already had its hands full policing album piracy in Asia and is scrambling to create new secured formats of its own.

But rather than stifle the recording industry, experts expect this technology, like VCRs in the 1980s, to create a whole new market for music. Already MTV Networks, hoping to cash in on the 17 million teens who make up its viewing audience, has numerous Web sites in the works, including Red Rocket (an online educational toy retailer) Imagine Radio (featuring customizable audio channels) SonicNet (a music-news site) and the Box (with cable music videos on demand). MTV is also launching qwert.com, a music site that will carry the usual information about stars but will allow users to program their own over-the-Web music station.

Meanwhile, the film industry is using a similar version of the audio MP3 format, MPEG2, to compress full-length movie features onto DVDs. The compressed data causes some distortions that can be detected by the trained eye, but most viewers do not notice the difference. The main technological problem is the time it takes a computer to download such a huge amount of information. Some movies take more than 12 hours. More troubling are the legal and ethical questions. The films are all pirated, new releases either stolen and then made available by someone inside the industry, the color labs or surreptitiously videotaped in a movie theater. They are then made available for free on so-called "underground" Web sites off the beaten path of the Internet and the World Wide Web, where copyright laws are not so easily enforced. So far, the studios insist that the quality of such pirated films is so bad that only a relatively small part of the market is willing to take the pains to download pilfered films. But the fact that such a market exists will surely further spur the industry to find ways to market its product over the Internet, making the nation's most popular and profitable theater the family living room.

How long can it be before the new hit song is "I want my MP3?" ■

Job Descriptions

EXAMPLE: E! ONLINE

above the line

EDITOR IN CHIEF Like his pre-digital print colleague, the top editor of a Web site oversees not only the editorial and art department personnel and ensures the quality of all writing and design, he also charts the course of electronic production and technology departments. Since a great site often inspires spinoff WWW sites, the successful editor in chief is likely to find himself in charge of multiple adjunct sites in addition to the "mother ship." He also works closely with business and new site development, marketing and advertising/sales departments. On the editorial side, he determines which features, columns, news stories, departments, games, online chats and Webcasts are appropriate for the site, working with staff editors to make assignments. He coordinates with the managing editor the scheduling of stories, taking into special account what appears on the "front page" of the site, which, unlike a static magazine cover, is changed frequently as new stories break. Calling the shots on what is given play on the front page is critical to bringing users back to the site and to ensuring the site remains accessible and easily navigated. The editor in chief also has responsibility for editorial budgeting and payroll.

PRESIDENT / CHIEF OPERATING OFFICER

Like the publisher in a magazine, the COO is in charge of the business and administrative side of site operations. Both marketing and advertising report directly to the COO. He or she also is responsible for developing and expanding the site's relationships with portal sites, consumer online services and content aggregators. For the COO, the bottom line is the bottom line: making the site profitable by creating multiple revenue streams and by strategically growing the business at a manageable pace and to a sustainable level.

CREATIVE DIRECTOR

An art director is an art director is an art director—no matter what the title. Fittingly, the Web site creative director invariably has transitioned from print media. He or she is responsible for creating the site's visual identity and must enrich it regularly while maintaining the overall look. In some ways, the creative director is constrained by limitations on designing for the Internet. In other ways, the designer has unprecedented freedom to utilize such techniques as animations, revolving pictures, rolling text, sound elements and interactive technology to enliven the visual presentation of the site's content. He or she constantly explores new techniques and applications to enhance that look and assigns designers to work on various large-scale projects and individual stories.

Job Descriptions

below the line

MANAGING EDITOR   The managing editor works with the editor in chief to schedule posting dates of all stories, then coordinates with the production, design, copy and marketing departments to ensure that the content is fully prepared when needed—down to the smallest detail. For example, the managing editor does final beta testing of content to ensure that all elements are in place and that the design and production of a story replicate equally well on Macintosh computers and on PCs, where type and images can be 40 percent larger. He or she makes sure all hyperlinks in stories are active and implements adjustments required for optimal distribution across all carriers. America Online users, for example, cannot access a full screen, so the managing editor replicates some editorial onto separate pages accessible to AOL users.

EXECUTIVE EDITOR The executive editor is the righthand man of the editor in chief, working to conceive features, assign and edit stories and department copy. He or she helps with quality control and oversees the smooth running of the staff while working closely with staff writers and freelancers, line editing and ensuring the accuracy of major editorial features.

NEWS EDITOR This individual oversees newswriting staff and coordinates breaking news coverage featured on the site—in the case of E! Online, any major studio shake-ups or leaks of significant deals. Accordingly, he or she is accountable for the accuracy and topicality of all stories. This is an especially pivotal position, since one of the great selling points of a Web site is its ability to report the news instantaneously, without waiting for printing or delivery hassles.

REVIEWS EDITOR This editor develops a nationwide network of freelance critics and coverage for the site's reviews of CDs, videos, computer equipment—whatever. Again, since a Web site "magazine" has to be literally up-to-the-minute, reviewers must not only understand the workings of their medium, but also be plugged-in enough to get in on the first looks and premieres.

ASSOCIATE EDITOR The associate editor assigns and edits departments and items that must be updated daily or weekly and coordinates with the copy editor and managing editor to ensure accuracy and timeliness of copy.

He or she secures deals for Web casts, chat sessions and live video feeds, arranges access to celebrities and other on-location interview subjects, secures credentials for staff, and schedules necessary ISDN and analog phone company lines. The events editor coordinates with the managing editor the development of editorial material tying in with live events and tracks site traffic during and after the event.

He or she reads all editorial material for spelling, punctuation, consistency and ensures it is consistent with house style. The copy editor codes all stories in basic HTML (boldface, italic, point size of typeface, headline color, etc.) and enters editorial material into the appropriate database for those sections of site that are database-driven.

DESIGNER The designer works under the creative director to create the layouts for feature stories and departments and designs the header graphics to communicate a story's overall feel, tone and intent. In the digital world, where the medium itself must be entertaining, successful designers must continuously push the boundaries of the medium by incorporating novel techniques and emerging technologies.

PHOTO EDITOR The photo editor secures all photographic material, including still photos, film and audio clips, to support the editorial content of the site, paying particular attention to securing all rights and clearances for the material to be used. Online publications are under unique constraints limiting their ability to use photos that are not technically in the public domain. Since a story posted on a Web site has no specific shelf life, as in, for example, a monthly print publication, visual material must be edited with an eye to longevity and the ability to sustain user interest for the long haul.

DIGITAL ARTIST

He or she processes graphics for daily updating of editorial, including "front-door" pictures that typically change daily. The digital artist also designs in-house ad banners for the marketing department and may maintain the production schedule for the design department.

SENIOR PRODUCER

The senior producer manages the production team which is responsible for the complex HTML coding as well as coding of Javascript and ASP. Producers also place content onto the site's servers. The senior producer is responsible for developing and realizing plans for maintaining the site's freshness, technical innovativeness and user interface. He or she works closely with the editor in chief, creative director and head of technology to ensure that the initiatives of editorial, design and technology departments come together in a logical, cohesive way.

PRODUCER

The producer works with the managing editor, line editor, copy editor and designer to build HTML-coded files into the appropriate sections of the site. He also works with ad sales and marketing staff to produce complex ads and contests, expedites content distribution, and acts as a project manager by securing various elements of a story (editorial, graphics, photos and captions, audio/video clips and technology) from respective departments where they are created and assembled in final form for posting on the site.

ASSOCIATE PRODUCER

In addition to assisting producers, the associate producer beta-tests and checks hyperlinks and animation in editorial. He also ensures that RealAudio, RealVideo and Quicktime files are operating properly on the site. He may maintain the daily production calendar.

The associate producer prepares all audio and video for use on the site and may coordinate games that appear on the site. He or she may also produce original video used in promos for the site.

This individual negotiates agreements with content partners (i.e., those sites and vendors such as WebTV, Snap, Wink, EchoStar, Roadrunner, MSN, WorldGate and Comcast, among others, that license and transmit the originating site's content to their users). He or she determines what content is available and how and when it will be distributed. This producer may also manage the promotion and propagation of areas on the site dedicated to e-commerce and other activities.

DIRECTOR, SYSTEMS / NETWORK ENGINEERING

This individual conceives overall direction of the site's technology organization, including component groups of systems/network, database and interactive content engineering. He or she also defines and implements technology strategy, oversees application of technology to meet both short- and long-term goals, develops relationships with third-party technology partners and vendors of products and services, and evaluates industry trends, technology, tools and applications.

SENIOR DATABASE ENGINEER

The database engineer maintains the site's underlying database, ensuring that database is always accessible. He also writes the script for data import and export, develops CGI text, performs preventative maintenance and writes tools to perform monitoring and consistency checks.

SENIOR SOFTWARE ENGINEER

The software engineer designs, codes and tests programs including Perl scripts, Java, Javascript and PRISM templates that support the Web site. (These programs allow users to access various screens on the site, to display information retrieved from the database and provide animated output for games.) He or she also develops other programs which the production department incorporates into the database and deals with the speed of user retrieval and animation quality. The software engineer may evaluate newly released software and backup programs and administer Y2K-compliance protocols.

SOFTWARE ENGINEER

This engineer provides back-end software support, including identifying and fixing "bugs," researching ways of enhancing user experience and evaluating new software.

DATABASE ADMINISTRATOR

The database administrator monitors database-space usage, makes recommendations for data speed/performance improvements, writes scripts to automate database backups, and creates and tests disaster recovery plans for database objects and data (tables, databases, indexes, screen views, etc.).

DIRECTOR, BUSINESS DEVELOPMENT

Reporting to the most senior executives, the person in this position is responsible for expanding the company's relationships with third parties for the purpose of achieving the primary business objectives of generating traffic and revenue. He or she establishes such relationships with portal sites, consumer online services and other content aggregators, and also researches and develops new revenue streams including international syndication and partnership agreements. The director advises executives on opportunities in emerging markets (e.g., interactive television) and works closely with the sales and marketing staffs on day-to-day business matters.

DIRECTOR, NEW SITE DEVELOPMENT

The new site development director conceives and implements adjunct sites that will enhance overall traffic, revenue and visibility of the "mother site," looking for ways to create synergy between the main site and spinoff sites. He or she also locates and identifies potential vendor partners and negotiates agreements with such partners.

NEW SITES EDITOR

This individual conceives and assigns all content related to adjunct sites, hires support staff where necessary and generates marketing copy that goes toward forging a strong association between the mother and adjunct site(s) in the minds of users.

NEW SITES MANAGER

The manager designs architecture to interface adjunct sites with the main site and develops deployment plans with software, graphic and database designers to integrate new vendor partners into the main site. He or she determines requirements for user interface and coordinates with the database administrator.

VICE PRESIDENT, MARKETING

The marketing VP drives traffic to the site and builds awareness of brand through traditional marketing methods including advertising, promotions, internal and external PR. He or she oversees ancillary functions (such as research and user satisfaction) and maximizes the relationship with the parent company as well as initiating and following through on relationships with various partners including AOL, Yahoo!, @Home and WebTV.

The marketing supervisor implements marketing programs and promotional strategies for main and affiliated sites to maximize brand identity and drive traffic to the sites. He or she cultivates existing partnerships with distribution and promotional partners, including AOL, WebTV, CompuServe, theglobe, Yahoo!, and Excite. He coordinates scheduling and placement of advertising and evaluates effectiveness of internal and external campaigns, and also supervises all elements of online contests, including rules, design and distribution of awards. In addition, the marketing supervisor researches and analyzes traffic patterns and site usage and tracks trends to support editorial, sales, e-commerce and new business.

MANAGER, ELECTRONIC COMMERCE This position manages and is responsible for strategic planning of the merchandising, operations, marketing, finance and production groups required to sustain an online commerce-enabled system.

He or she ensures that all customer service needs are met and conceives and implements new navigational features to build traffic and user retention. The CD manager develops support systems, including automatic response forms and FAQ templates, and oversees responses to user queries.

The support coordinator tests the user interface to ensure that user experience is as smooth and enjoyable as possible, and responds to user correspondence, bug reports and feedback. He or she writes a weekly newsletter that provides a primary connection to the site and often drives traffic in the front door.

PUBLIC RELATIONS DIRECTOR

The PR director develops strategies for promotion of the site content and online personalities and represents the site at trade shows and related events. He or she also manages the PR department and personnel.

PUBLIC RELATIONS COORDINATOR

He or she composes and distributes press releases and media alerts and pitches content, talent and executive interviews to consumer broadcast and print media outlets. This person coordinates the development of online talent image (including personal appearance itineraries), manages and updates PR databases and responds to requests for press kits as well as coordinating photo shoots and materials duplication.

ADVERTISING DIRECTOR The AD manages day-to-day relationships with advertisers and sponsors and represents the site to external advertising customers. He or she generates and maintains new and existing business for the site.

ADVERTISING TRAFFIC COORDINATOR This person is the liaison between the ad sales, production and technology departments and handles all aspects of an advertiser's campaign (except the actual sale of online space), which may range from basic banners to full sponsorship of a live, online event. He or she works with clients or their advertising agencies to secure ad materials and then enters them into site's system. Post-campaign, the ATC follows up with clients and tracks ad effectiveness.

theater

Reanimated along solidly G-rated lines, Broadway these days has become kind of an amusement attraction in itself, Playland, as it were. It's where both serious patrons and tourists alike can take in anything from intellectually stimulating dramas to long-running lavishly produced musicals while soaking up the ambience of the birthplace to some of the greatest theater of the 20th century. So it should come as no surprise that Disney has landed on the Great White Way, making it one more hub of its global empire with blockbuster musicals like *Beauty and the Beast* and *The Lion King*—and bringing back to life New York's famed 42nd Street in the bargain.

The New York theater scene today may be viewed as a net importer of cultural goods, whether shipped in from the bright lights of London's West End or box offices of Anytown, USA. It's perhaps only natural that *The Lion King*, one of Broadway's biggest hits in years, began life in the animation studios of Burbank, California.

It is the most visible sign that the stage has been subsumed into the cross-cultural, multidisciplinary—sometimes seemingly gaseous—world of global entertainment, where properties have become like alien shape-shifters straight out of *Star Trek*, beginning as a film, transmogrifying into a recording, then translated to a site on the World Wide Web. But there is a difference. In a sophisticated universe of digital production and fiber-optic networks, theater remains a decidedly low-tech business—a primordial oasis of sweat, flesh and faith.

It was little more than 30 years ago that Simon and Garfunkle aped the question that was agonizing '60s New York's cultural cognoscenti: "Is the theater really dead?" While the movie industry had been hit hard by the arrival of television, theater fared even worse, having taken a one-two punch from both TV and rock 'n' roll. The popularization of television, which transported audience-friendly vaudeville and burlesque to the small screen, had cut deeply into theater box office. The film industry responded to the threat of TV by releasing big-budget, multilocation epics, historical dramas and "event" movies with the vaunted "cast of thousands." But in America, with the exception of pop-rock extravaganzas like *Jesus Christ Superstar*, the theater remained a human-scaled, hand-cranked medium, dependent on the original voices of its authors scattered across the nation for its vitality.

The fact is that the theater had always been essentially different from its later progeny, film and television. It had never had the deep-pocketed studios or networks to feed and care for it. Playmaking had been, and continued to be, basically a local enterprise, supported by generous patrons and avid theatergoers of hundreds of small, not-for-profit theaters and theater groups across the country. From Boston to Pasadena, these locals groomed and nurtured up-and-coming playwrights like David Mamet and David Rabe, staging both new plays and classic revivals in venues varying from 50 seats to 1,000.

Many small plays that were first produced on regional stages, like Marsha Norman's '*Night, Mother* and August Wilson's *Fences*, found commercial backing and made the jump to New York or took to the road in touring companies. But on Broadway, bigger has almost always been better: By 1980, the quintessence of success in Times Square was Gower Champion's *42nd Street*, a tap-happy celebration of a theatrical era gone by.

By the late '80s and '90s, a new generation of impresarios like writer/composer Cameron Mackintosh, Andrew Lloyd Webber and Garth Drabinsky sought a way to compete with movies by staging such superbudget, special-effects-laden, theater-as-event shows as *Miss Saigon*, *The Phantom of the Opera*, *Les Misérables* and *Ragtime*. Broadway rebounded in terms of the quantity and scale of shows being produced, if not necessarily in quality. Broadway was once again generally a profitable bet for producers hoping to recoup their money onstage.

Theater, after all, had one thing going for it the other performing arts did not: stars within, well, spitting distance. (Many a front-row patron, in fact, has literally been within the spray zone of a robustly articulate Shakespearean.) Where else could one see live, big-name, sometimes almost mythic, performers appearing nightly? Dustin Hoffman, Meryl Streep, Al Pacino, Dame Judith Dench— were turning up on the Broadway boards regularly and, in recent years, even on small, regional stages. For one thing, the stage is almost an irresistible narcotic to "serious" actors. Many trained for the stage continued to be drawn to it, despite salary caps well below the seven-figure fees Hollywood trades in. At its best, theater truly is an art form that affords its practitioners and audiences alike a deep understanding of what it means to be alive. Simultaneously highly disciplined yet intuitively human, theater is a living, breathing creature with the power to unnerve and inspire.

The draw of star power notwithstanding, what keeps American theater off the ventilator and sustains it as a vibrant life force and invaluable part of American culture is its essentially democratic nature. Like the poet, the mentality of the theater artist is typically one of alienation from conventional society. Effectively locked out of highly homogenized Hollywood, gays and lesbians, ethnic and minority artists and social "outcasts" of every kind find a creative home in the world of theater. Though some of the work, as with any other medium, proves to be limited, flawed or even self-serving, truly original voices can and do find a world that supports them, ultimately bringing to life such works as *M. Butterfly*, *Angels in America* and *Side Man*—commercial hits which would never have found a place in the movies or on television.

Theater is also unique in that it is the only one of the entertainment arts with an underlying support group—both public and private—dedicated to its survival and growth.The debate surrounding the role of government subsidy for nonprofit theater drones on, but support from foundations, corporations and individual patrons has played a pivotal role in expanding the art beyond the at times almost suffocatingly hothouse of the New York scene. Today, very original work is being conceived and produced in regional theaters all over America. Every year in New York, Chicago and Los Angeles, professional "99-seat" theaters and "showcase" productions by the hundreds offer low-priced tickets to adventuresome audiences and new opportunities for playwrights, actors and directors to hone their work.

Unlike the film business, which is centered in Hollywood and controlled by a handful of studios, theater is a decentralized, even far flung industry. Presently, 134 theaters are members of the Theatre Communications Group, selling more than 11 million tickets a year. So influential were the regionals that the American Theatre Critics Association was formed back in 1974 in order to cover the vast number of quality productions playing in cities from San Francisco to off-Broadway.

"Overnight success" stories in the film industry are the stuff Hollywood is made of. Everyone from film-school students to the power-lunch crowd knows the tale of the unknown screenwriter with a half-finished script who wanders into an agent's office or happens to sit down to dinner next to a producer and 24 hours later has a seven-figure development deal. The truth is, with the right project at the right time, even a wanna-be can follow a fairly defined path from agent to producer to studio to find success—though, of course, the trick is having that one-in-a-million idea and even then the road is infinitely complex and tenuous. The theater business has no such putative road—not even a mythic yellow-brick trail. For one thing, there is no theater studio system, no entertainment entity searching for, buying and developing hundreds of plays to be produced onstage. Instead, there are commercial theaters, some theater production companies like the erstwhile Livent and an undefined pool of potential investors willing to sink their money into the crapshoot of commercial theater production.

The vast majority of plays begin as workshop projects or not-for-profit ventures in regional theaters. These theaters, privately and publically endowed, are simply hoping to recoup a percentage of their production costs and operating expenses at the box office. These ventures are about the "art" of theater. An extended family of dedicated theater lovers—volunteers, professionals willing to work for scale and devoted "show people" of all walks—keep these theaters alive.

A small percentage of these regional plays will find an audience and an interest from a big-name producer or director dedicated to finding financial backing for the production, which is then honed usually in a succession of larger venues. When that "one-in-a-million" play does make it to Broadway, it will have been rewritten, revised and polished, cast, staged and performed hundreds of times in a number of regional theaters. Many times the original backers, producers, directors and actors are long gone before the play turns its first dollar of profit.

The Tony Award-winning *Side Man*, for instance, began as a reading at the West Bank Cafe in New York City presented by the Naked Angels theater group. New York stage and film artistic director Peter Manning "discovered" the play. With a grant from the Weissberger Foundation, Manning workshopped the not-for-profit play at the Classic Stage Company Theater, continuing to rewrite and polish the drama. The play drew good critic reviews and Manning decided to take it commercial, bringing aboard producer Joan Stein and renting and producing the play first at Broadway's Roundabout Theater and, finally, at its critically acclaimed run at the Golden Theater.

Such a route may seem a classic journey from art to commercial success, but at the same time *Side Man* was being developed, another Tony winner, Disney's *The Lion King* was following a wholly different path. Instead of a basement reading, *The Lion King* was born as an animated feature. Backed by the Walt Disney Company empire, the challenge was not finding commercial backing but in translating a story from the virtual world of animation into a three-act play which could be performed live on a finite stage with real actors, not computer-generated images and artists' renderings. Though perhaps not as humanly revealing or

emotionally profound as *Side Man*, the cutting-edge technical innovation, and costume design by director Julie
Taymor was no less stunning in its expanding the limits of
what modern theater—and the imagination—can attain.

Which all goes to show, as another famous playwright
observed 400 years ago, that in the end, when it comes to
critical or commercial success, "the play's the thing." ∎

Job Descriptions

above the line

**PRODUCER /
ARTISTIC DIRECTOR**

What's the difference between a producer and artist director? One smokes cigars, the other doesn't. Actually, the difference comes down to money. In commercial theater, the producer finds the project, acquires the rights, raises the money and selects the venue. In non-profit theater, the artistic director serves a similar function, except that the venue is fixed. The artistic director anticipates that he or she will lose money and seeks government, corporate and private subsidies. The commercial producer looks for a "vehicle" that can make a profit. With current Broadway smashes such as *The Lion King* making profits in excess of a three-quarters-of-a-million-dollar weekly draw at the box office, it's easy to see what kind of financial muscle is needed to mount a show on the Great White Way. The non-profit regional theaters, on the other hand, earn less than half of their revenue from box-office receipts. Both require great knowledge, charm and top-level schmoozing techniques.

DIRECTOR

Although theater is commonly referred to as an "actors' medium" the stage director is arguably just as important to the process. While the stage director cannot manipulate a performance after the fact by editing the film, he/she has primary responsibility for insuring that the story is clearly told and that the pace of the performance is varied enough to hold an audience's attention. The director is responsible for coming up with the concept or interpretation of a play and works closely with the designers to execute his or her vision. In new works, the director is also a collaborator with the playwright, often suggesting changes in the text to clarify the action or make a character's actions more believable or more compelling to watch. After casting the play, which some will argue is 90 percent of the director's job, the most important task is staging, or "blocking." the play—that is, determining where and when the actors will move about on the stage. The director organizes and conducts rehearsals and makes sure the play is ready by opening night. Before the late-19th century, the great leading actors of the day, their repertoire of parts already committed to memory, would go on with one rehearsal. A new actor signed on to perform a familiar Shakespeare play might simply inquire if the playing of the part involved "the usual moves." The idea of creating a fresh interpretation and a coherent, unified artistic concept for repertory plays was unheard of. A few directors today are seen as *auteurs;* among them, Joseph Chaikin, Anne Bogart, Andrei Serban, Robert Wilson and Peter Sellars. They are known for a specific style of staging, use of technical and scenic effects, or of demanding a uniform style of performance from the actors. Usually the director simply aspires to "serve the text" and create the style that most closely matches the playwright's intent. Director Robert Falls, who is also the artistic director of Chicago's non-profit Goodman Theater, scored a commercial hit directing the Tony Award-wining production of *Death of a Salesman*. After that, the Walt Disney Company hired him to direct their new musical, *Aïda*, written by Elton John and Tim Rice. A part of the deal, the Goodman's subscribers were promised preferred seating for the commercial show.

Job Descriptions

below the line

CASTING DIRECTOR   Big productions and the larger theater companies employ casting directors to help the director sort though the submissions of pictures and résumés by actors, their agents and managers. A casting director is informed of the director's interpretation of the play and how he or she wants to go with a particular role, i.e., the range of physical and personality attributes of actor desired. The casting director sends out breakdowns of the available roles in the play based on a careful reading of the script. The leading roles in a major commercial production are usually cast early in the process to insure box-office viability. The casting director's job is to make sure the best actors are seen by the director before the final decisions are made.

ASSISTANT DIRECTOR

An assistant director is often an apprentice director. The AD helps organize the rehearsal schedule, takes acting and production notes and may conduct some extra rehearsals with the actors.

PRODUCTION MANAGER

The production manager serves as a liaison between the producer, the director, the designers and the theater facility.

SET DESIGNER

Once a director has decided on an interpretation for a play, the set designer is called upon to create the necessary scenic effects. The best set designers are sensitive to the emotional effects a play is intended to have on the audience and will design the set accordingly. Although aesthetic effects are of paramount importance, the practical aspects of a set are essential for the success of a production. Every care must be made to ensure that scene changes can be achieved quickly and unobtrusively and that the set itself is "actor-friendly."

COSTUME DESIGNER

An actor may look in the mirror on opening night and, seeing herself in costume for the first time, really connect with that sense of "otherness" for the first time. Like the set designer, a costume designer's first duties are to the director and the play (usually in that order). If *Measure for Measure* is to be set in the antebellum South, then the designer must know everything about the attire of the period and bring that knowledge to bear upon the task of fitting the character to a particular set of clothes. The best designers inhabit the characters of the play nearly as much the actors themselves in order to select the most appropriate attire. The color and design scheme must be coordinated with the set designer in consultation with the director to create a coherent visual effect.

STITCHERS

The stitcher works closely with the costume designer to assemble and sew both male and female attire to be used in the play. He or she also does the tucks, letting-out and alterations marked by the cutter/fitters on all rented costumes to specifically fit the actors wearing the clothes.

WARDROBE MISTRESS

Once the play is ready for performance, the wardrobe mistress takes care of costume maintenance: repairs, cleaning, ironing and replacement of lost or irretrievably damaged articles of clothing.

DRESSER

Name actors are privileged to be served by a dresser in a large budget production. The dresser helps the actor get ready for the play, arranging the costumes in the dressing room, seeing that everything is in order for the night's performance and assisting with costume changes.

MAKEUP ARTIST / WIG MASTER

In less elaborate productions, actors are expected to apply their own makeup and take care of hairpieces, wigs and facial hair. In a production such as *Beauty and the Beast* or *The Lion King*, where cast members appear as animals, expert help is required. Even a one-man show such as *Mark Twain Tonight* required a lengthy visit to the makeup chair before Hal Holbrook appeared onstage as the elder American man of letters.

LIGHTING DESIGNER

There is an expression that "mood" is merely "doom" spelled backwards for the actor. In a sense this is true, for any actor who uses his or her voice to create a kind of generalized emotional atmosphere will be laughed off the stage. While actors are charged with pursuing the action of the play, the lighting designer is free to create the moods that will enhance those actions and moments in a play. Perhaps this is one of the most rewarding aspects of performing live. A film actor is conscious of achieving truthful behavior in a scene but cannot feel the effect of the entire production on the audience. A stage actor is usually aware of the change in lighting and of the sense of being a part of the total picture presented to the spectator. The lighting designer has the power to literally "color" an actor's performance. The designer also has the responsibility of adequately illuminating the sets and costumes. Not unlike a motion-picture director of photography, the designer has be sure that the audience's eyes are drawn to the right places on stage by focusing or aiming the instruments according to the director's needs.

SOUND DESIGNER

A relative newcomer to the art of theater, the sound designer has the primary task of orchestrating recorded sound effects and music for a production. Part of the job may entail arranging the speakers around the stage and in the house and setting the volume levels to create the sensations of depth and realism.

STAGE MANAGER The stage manager sits beside the director in rehearsal, writes down the blocking, records any script changes, makes notes about technical cues, costumes, props, the sets and the stage furniture. In short, the stage manager must know everything there is to know in order to run the show from beginning to end: calling for light and sound cues, set changes and making sure the actors are in their places at the top of each scene. After the play opens, it is the stage manager who is responsible for making sure the play runs the way the director directed it. The stage manager rehearses the under-studies and replacement actors when necessary.

RUNNING CREW / STAGEHANDS In big commercial theaters, stage-hands are union employees and earn respectable salaries for hefting the set pieces around, pulling the curtains and oper-ating backstage machinery. In lesser venues, unpaid interns or even the actors themselves are employed to change the set behind the curtain or during a blackout between scenes.

PROP MASTER

An inappropriate prop can ruin a scene, and the severest theater critic can skewer a play over a bungled bit of stage business or a prop that calls too much attention to itself. While playing a role, an actor may be called upon to handle a cigarette while walking and talking, wave a fan flirtatiously in a Restoration comedy, eat food that looks fit for a king, smash a plate over someone's head, hurl a book across the stage, threaten someone with a knife or gun, write a letter, read a letter, take a letter out of an envelope using a letter opener, burn a letter, fold a pile of shirts or put fresh flowers in a vase. The prop master is called upon to make sure the commonplace implements of everyday life function in an everyday way, that cigarette lighters light eight times a week and that the actor playing George Washington isn't packing heat with a Smith & Wesson (unless the playwright or director wants it that way, of course).

TECHNICAL DIRECTOR

The technical director, or TD, as he or she is apt to be referred to, is responsible for overseeing the construction of the sets by the carpenters, the hanging of the lights by the master electrician and execution of the overall technical requirements of the play. The TD is a kind of "reality check," advising the director and designers about the feasibility of their plans in a particular theater. Most technical directors are ingenious when it comes to mechanical improvisation, for in many productions the dreams of the designers and directors are at odds with the reality of the budget.

SOUND OPERATOR Taking cues from the stage manager and keeping a watchful eye on the action of the play, the sound operator runs the tape or digital playback machine during the performance. The sound operator is responsible for adjusting volume levels of microphones used by the performers. In virtually all musicals, the actors are "miked."

LIGHT BOARD OPERATOR Computers have dramatically reduced the workload of the light board operator while increasing the expectations of the director and lighting designer. Elaborate lighting changes involving dozens of instruments can be executed at the touch of a button. But the cues still have to be taken off the action onstage and a light change may have to be held if a piece of machinery slows down a set change or if an actor is late for a cue.

FIGHT DIRECTOR

The success of action films have all but mandated that live stage fights be expertly choreographed by a fight director, sometimes referred to as a coordinator of choreographer. The popularity of classical plays set in the days of sword fights has created a substantial demand for this expertise. While most graduate school actors are trained in the fundamentals of stage fighting and swordplay, the design of a fight and the optimal use of playing area are best left to a fight director.

CHOREOGRAPHER

The great dance choreographers have played a central role in creating exciting musical theater. Musical theater is, in a very real sense, America's classical theater, with its universal themes and heightened forms of physical and vocal expression. The choreographer helps to tell the story of the play and provide the visual dimension to the music. The big ensemble numbers draw attention to the choreographer's skill and inventiveness, while the one- and two-person songs require sensitive, character-driven stage movement.

Most resident theater companies have a dramaturge or literary manager to serve as a sort of gatekeeper for the large number of plays received by the theater every year from both aspiring and established playwrights. Such a post may be filled by a faculty member at a local university. Most theaters receive some of their grant money based on their commitment to developing new works by local or American playwrights and the dramaturge is often a key player in the organization of readings and workshops of new plays. Major recent works, such as *Angels in America* and *The Kentucky Cycle*, were born and nurtured by regional theaters.

radio

Way back in 1919, an AT&T executive proposed a novelty system by which customers could push a button number on the telephone and access any kind of amusement they wanted over the phone line—the first notion that a user could "download" an individualized audio file delivered over a phone line. Three years later, in 1922, AT&T cooked up the radiotelephone, a "phone booth of the air" composed of 38 radio stations linked by the company's long lines. For a fee, programmers could broadcast to telephone customers and charge the same rate as a normal station-to-station call. AT&T would not be involved in the creation of content any more than it was concerned with what someone making a phone call had to say. Though the radiophone never got off the ground, the concept of selling airtime was born forever.

From its roots, radio was perceived as an innovative, limitless medium of mass communication. Long before the advent of the Internet, it was seen as the ultimate democratic form of communication, with myriad stations providing an endless array of music, drama and discussion representing a full complement of tastes that was the closest thing to customized programming a for-profit, general-interest business could hope to attain. And it was all free. All you needed to enjoy it was a $10 transistor radio. No ISP fee, no downloading charge, no disc.

Among the media elite today, of course, broadcast radio evokes all the spin of the ham radio operator. Media-meisters talk about an around-the-corner future where Web surfers transform their PCs into personal jukeboxes, audiophiles carry downloaded playlists on Visa card-sized flash cards, and Web sites like Broadcast.com dominate the virtual airways with near limitless listening options. Meanwhile, radio conjures images of DJs surrounded by mad scientist-sized vacuum tubes or Frasier-like aquarium broadcast booths.

In truth, new media's strength lies in the size of its stock shares. Real end-of-day profits are minimal or nonexistent. The market is betting on the future of the digital world. Radio, however clunky its image, is for the most part deep in the black. The Arbitron Company, which measures radio audiences in 270 markets, estimated that up to 98 percent of all Americans over the age of 12 listen to radio at least once a week. The United States has 12,560 radio stations, the majority commercially run "formats" offering around-the-clock programming. In Los Angeles, the nation's Number one radio market in terms of annual revenue, the number of people driving in cars and listening to the radio between 4 p.m. and 5 p.m. is equal to the entire population of Atlanta. According to Cincinnati-based research firm Duncan's American Radio, in 1998, the country's largest radio company, AMFM, generated $1.84 billion, with 464 stations. The nation's five largest radio companies together earned $4.5 billion.

All a broadcaster needs is a mike, a soundproof booth and a broadcasting tower. Advertising rates, however, can run to the thousands of dollars for a 30-second spot. It is the reason the large entertainment conglomerates own radio networks as part of their portfolios. In 1999, the Walt Disney company, which owns, among others, Los Angeles-based KLOS-FM, was embarrassed by employee harassment lawsuits which charged that a promotion campaign called "The Black 'Ho" run on its top-rated morning drive time show with DJs, Mark and Brian, was racially insensitive. When civil rights groups protested, critics charged Disney was reluctant to react because the "Mark and Brian" show alone brought in $24 million a year.

■ ■ ■

From its outset, radio revolutionized the entertainment business. The rise of radio networks in the 1920s and '30s brought big-city entertainment into the homes of millions for the first time in history. Comedies, dramas, variety shows, symphony orchestras, operas and big bands were available to millions free of charge. The large tube radios occupied a revered place in the American life, replacing the fireplace as the symbolic center of the hearth. It would reach the zenith of its Golden Age in the 1930s, during the Great Depression, when President Roosevelt used the medium to reach into every household and calm the nation's fears with his "Fireside Chats." The radio networks quickly created the organizational and business model for entertainment broadcasting in America: predominantly advertiser-supported, privately run and competitive.

After a decade of rapid and, at times, chaotic expansion, the government stepped in to regulate the nascent industry in 1928, when the Coolidge Administration established the Federal Radio Commission, later renamed the Federal Communications Commission, or FCC. The small bureaucracy, originally housed in a small office in the Department of Commerce, issued licenses, established technical standards and assigned call letters and frequencies. Stations west of the Mississippi were assigned call letters beginning with K; those to the east began with W. International agreements assigned Canadian stations with the initial letter C; Mexican-owned stations with X.

In the early 1950s, the radio industry suffered its first crisis when the coming of television erased the medium's prestige and advertisers took their dollars and programs to the small screen. Radio's survival in the age of television depended on a number of programming and technological innovations. Chief among them was the local music and news format and the rise of the disc jockey show, generally credited to radio entrepreneurs Robert Todd Storz and Gordon McLendon.

In Dallas, McLendon revolutionized the business, introducing such innovations as local news, promotional giveaways and the "personality" disc jockey who could attract a loyal audience and give the local station an identity. A station manager at Omaha's local station, KOWH, Storz one night noticed that customers at a local bar tended to play the same songs over and over at the jukebox. He returned to the station and reworked the station's entire programming, replaying the most popular songs throughout the day, giving the audience what it wanted and at the same time "inventing" the Top 40 format.

Meanwhile, several cultural and technological forces converged in the 1950s to "save" radio. As the TV networks strove to appeal to the widest possible demographic, many cash-strapped local stations tried to appeal to specialized audiences. Already, early rhythm-and-blues programs carried "race" music across country and state lines late at night over the 50,000-watt clear channel AM stations like WLAC in Nashville. When rock 'n' roll suddenly emerged as a cultural phenomenon among teenagers, it was ready-made for radio. For one thing, the African-American-influenced rock was deemed too raw for national television audiences, leaving the entire genre to the radio industry, notwithstanding Elvis Presley's truncated appearance on the *Ed Sullivan Show*. At the same time, Motorola's invention of the automobile radio, pioneered in the 1940s, became a technological centerpiece of the "rebellious" teen culture, providing young adults with a means of listening to all the rock 'n' roll they wanted while cruising in their hot rods. "Drive time" radio was born, the ultimate jackpot for radio broadcasters and the mainstay of the entire radio indus-try today.

Another technological innovation helped the indus-try: the transistor radio. Overnight, radio was brought into the kitchen, the garage, the beach, even under the bed covers for late-night listening. By the 1960s, personality music radio caught fire and local DJs became household names in their communities: Joe Niagra on WIBG in Philadelphia, Robert W. Morgan on KHJ in Los Angeles, Arnie "Woo-Woo" Ginsburg on WMEX in Boston, Dan Ingram on New York's WABC, and Dick Biondi on WLS in Chicago, to name a few of the legends. Taking their cue from the intimate announcing style pioneered by CBS radio's Arthur Godfrey, personalities created unique one-on-one relationships with their listeners. Their ad-libbed patter matched the energy of rock music and seemed to fit the frenetic pace of urban life. Other formats came along to satisfy different audiences: new age, country and western, rhythm and blues, jazz, classical, talk and news as well as ethnic programming.

FM radio, invented in the 1930s, exploded in the 1960s with the coming of artist groups like the Beatles who didn't focus on creating one or two Top 40 hits but entire albums of quality cuts. The FM stations appealed to the first generation of audiophiles who disdained the commercialism of pop AM stations, introducing high-fidelity stereo sound to radio. The number of radio stations doubled as popular music formats migrated to the more prestigious FM venues. FM underground rock stations, KSAN-FM in San Francisco, KPPC-FM in Pasadena, California, and WBCN-FM in Boston overtook their AM Top 40 competitors and, in turn, became just as commercial. By the mid-1980s, AM radio's decline in popularity seemed irreversible. The more heavily populated radio spectrum became increasingly devoted to niche formats, catering to myriad tastes and interests. Where a top AM station in the '60s might command a 25 share of the total listening audience, by the 1980s, the number one station might lead with a mere 4.0 share.

The business remained as such until the Reagan Administration rescinded the so-called Fairness Doctrine, an FCC regulation requiring a radio station to offer equal time for the airing of opposing viewpoints. The foundation was laid for talk radio. The first of the radio pundits was conservative host Rush Limbaugh, who pulled in a consistently high audience share with a three-hour daily dose of folksy conservative philosophy and commentary. Hundreds of content-starved AM stations snapped up his satellite-delivered syndicated show and its corresponding ratings. Limbaugh's influence was so pervasive that by 1994, he was credited with having played a major role in helping elect the Republican majority to Congress.

Conglomerization came to the radio industry in the wake of the Telecommunications Act of 1996, which removed ownership restrictions for broadcasters, allowing one company to own up to eight stations in a market and removing the limit on the number of stations that could be owned nationally. The process of consolidation took on a frantic pace as a handful of large companies scrambled to secure as many stations as possible in the time-honored practice of vertical integration. It was an attempt to control both the supply, or programming, and the distribution, or radio signals. The process of consolidation took on a frantic pace as smaller companies merged and the industry's giants began cruising for smaller companies to swallow, in an old-fashioned attempt at vertical integration to control both supply (i.e., programming) and distribution (i.e., radio signals). By 1999, broadcast franchises Viacom and Infinity/CBS had merged, quickly followed by the proposed merger of AMFM and Clearchannel to create a behemoth controlling some 900 stations in markets blanketing the country.

The efficiencies of scale and multiple-station ownership made it possible for one operator to deliver 30 to 40 percent of a radio audience in a market to advertisers. This new profit potential has given Wall Street new interest in the radio business.

The trend has yielded both good and bad dividends. Radio revenues are up, but so are debt obligations created by the huge mergers and acquisitions. By most accounts, corporate culture is taking over at local stations. The number of commercial spots has increased and the music formats have become more risk-averse. Pop music stations concentrate their efforts at attracting the most lucrative demographic group of adults 25-54 years old. Syndication deals made competitive by satellite technology perfected in the 1980s continue to multiply. Conservative talk radio predominates both the local and the syndicated AM market.

There is now much speculation as to the future form of radio. Experiments in subscriber cable radio proved to be a disappointment to investors in the 1980s. The prospect of commercially uninterrupted music programming proved not enough incentive for most listeners to cough up a monthly fee. The idea of subscriber radio has not been abandoned, however. And once again, the automobile culture lies at the base.

In 1997, the FCC auctioned off the Digital Radio Services to two companies, presently known as CD Radio and XM Satellite Radio. Beginning in 2001, each company will offer approximately 100 channels to subscribers equipped with special radios. This satellite-delivered broadcasting service is primarily aimed at the mobile listener, designed to allow a driver crossing North America to remain tuned to the same channel from coast to coast. Uninterrupted "line-of-sight" transmission, boosted by terrestrial repeaters, will boost reception in urban and mountainous areas. The developers are gambling people will fork over the expense of after-market car radios capable of picking up satellite broadcasts. XM Satellite Radio hired the research firm Critical Mass Media to gauge the public's response to the new system. Researchers reported that 34 million listeners would be willing to pay $400 for a new radio and a $10 monthly subscription fee.

Meanwhile, radio and the Internet, by all appearances, seem headed for some kind of economic or technological collision in the near future. Most likely, that head-on meeting will take the form of of some kind of merger. Already, the Internet is carrying radio broadcasting. How long will it be before the wizards of Silicon Valley figure out a way to translate radio waves into the digital universe? ■

Job Descriptions

EXAMPLE: NPR(National Public Radio)
"All Things Considered"

GENERAL MANAGER The general manager oversees all aspects of the radio station's operation. In today's deregulated environment, the GM is apt to be running three or four stations in a market and hires the rest of the staff. In smaller markets, he or she is out selling the station with the account executives. In non-commercial radio, the GM must develop and maintain sources of funding and, in many cases, keep on good terms with the affiliated college or university.

SALES MANAGER

The sales manager may work under the general sales manager or local sales manager, depending on the size of the station and the market. The GSM may be in charge of handling agency buyers and selling the station to national advertisers. The sales manager supervises the account executives and coordinates the effort to win the business of local clients.

**PROGRAM DIRECTOR /
DIRECTOR OF OPERATIONS**

With the right kind of programming, a station can attract a large segment of the target audience. A soft-rock station may be targeted at attracting young females, age 18-34. A talk station may be predominantly male listeners ages 35-54. The PD must hire the right kind of air talent to appeal to that audience. The PD is responsible for the way the station sounds on the air and how the different elements (such as jingles, promotional announcements, commercials and music) are arranged. Public stations are increasingly aware of the need to appeal to the right people in order to increase membership and develop corporate underwriting.

MUSIC DIRECTOR This is an all-important job for the modern rock, hip-hop, contemporary hits or any station whose reputation depends on playing the best new music. The music director meets with record-company representatives every week to hear the latest releases. The MD selects the music best suited for the target audience. The MD uses computer programs to catalog and track what the station plays. Many stations are now fully digital and run music, commercials, jingles, promos and even prerecorded DJ "voice tracks" off the hard drive of a computer. At many stations, the MD doubles as a full-time air personality.

TRAFFIC MANAGER Once the account executive writes an order, the commercials have to be scheduled to go on the air. The traffic manager keeps track of the inventory, making sure that all spots run at the right times. The information is entered on the program log, indicating the length of the spot and the time it runs. The log tells the air talent or board operator when to play the spot, and other details, such as whether it is a recorded or "live" and the length. Sometimes a program feature is sponsored and needs a 10-second live "billboard" announcement before or after it is aired. Other spots may be sold as adjacencies to a popular feature. The sponsor is paying the station according to the estimated size of the audience, so the traffic manager must be sure that the spots run in the correct "day parts."

NEWS DIRECTOR
On a contemporary music station, the news director is often a one-person news department, he or she being the person that gets up at 3:30 a.m. to prepare the news for the morning drive. At a news/talk or all-news station, the news director supervises a team of in-studio anchors and field reporters.

PUBLIC SERVICE DIRECTOR /COMMUNITY RELATIONS
All stations are required by their licenses to serve their communities. The public service director may also be the news director or an overnight DJ's second job, someone the station coaxed into opening all the mail requesting free on-air community announcements. The better stations take the job seriously enough to air public service programs and announcements.

MARKETING DIRECTOR / PROMOTIONS

Marketing and promotions is a key department for a radio station in a competitive market. The director of marketing and/or promotions keeps up the station's visibility in the community through talent appearances, contests, giveaways and advertising in other media. Many urban contemporary and pop/rock stations hire "street teams" whose job it is to pop up in a station van at community events, store openings, concerts and schools and give away T-shirts, hats and bumper stickers as well as phone in reports to the station.

WEB MASTER

The Internet is an increasingly valuable marketing tool for many radio stations. Some stations broadcast on the Net, allowing people from around the world to tune in. On-air announcements can direct listeners to the station's Web site to send e-mail to the air talent or participate in promotion. The visual dimension of the Web is an important added benefit for sponsors. The Web master oversees the design and maintenance of the site.

ACCOUNT EXECUTIVE Account executives are responsible for selling the station's airtime, typically in 60- or 30-second increments known as "spots."The AE proposes a plan for a prospect that demonstrates how advertising on the station can improve the business. This job has been limited to commercial radio stations. Recently, however, one Los Angeles public station put a classified in a local trade newsletter seeking to fill such a position, providing more evidence of the blurring distinctions between commercial and non-commercial, or public, radio.

DIRECTOR OF DEVELOPMENT Public radio stations hire a director of development to woo corporate underwriting for specific programs, projects and for the station as a whole. Typically, such sponsors are mentioned in 10-second "billboard" announcements at the beginning and end of programs they help pay for. Such arrangements have long been a common practice among commercial radio stations. All that's missing is the 30 or 60 second spot.

The voices heard on the radio create impressions that can last in the listener's mind for a lifetime. The air talent plays many roles at a station, including news anchor, reporter, radio personality or DJ, talk show host, traffic reporter, production voice or straight announcer. Major syndicated talents such as Rush Limbaugh, Dr. Laura Schlessinger, Howard Stern and Don Imus command annual salaries in the millions. A popular morning person in a medium market such as Cincinnati may make a very comfortable six-figure salary. Most air talents work odd hours for low to mediocre pay. Those talents not destined to star in a high-profile morning show or a top-15 market may graduate to sales and management jobs.

PRODUCTION DIRECTOR

In today's increasingly automated music radio environment, the production director has an increasingly important task of selling, or "imaging" a station in the listener's mind. He or she may also be the "voice" of the station, reading the promotional announcements in addition to editing the music and sound effects. Some stations hire a production announcer specifically to voice the promotional spots.

CHIEF ENGINEER The chief engineer keeps the station on the air, maintaining the technical logs and the station's equipment. He or she is required to have a first class radiotelephone license, issued by the FCC to those who pass a rigorous technical exam.

BOARD OPERATOR Basically a button pusher, the board operator's job can be a challenging one nevertheless. This person sitting "behind the glass" has been a fixture in radio since its earliest days. Except at unionized stations, DJs run their own boards, cueing CDs, records, tapes or clicking a mouse to advance to the next commercial or song. Talk stations require a board op to play the commercials and maintain the programming and technical log for the on-air host.

CALL SCREENER The call screener is a very important person in talk radio and may also be employed by top music radio personalities who put phone calls from listeners on the air. The screener asks a caller what he or she wants to say on the air, then types a short summary on to a computer screen for the host to read. Confused, inarticulate, or repeat callers are usually asked to call back another time.

PRODUCER Producers book guest interviews for talk-show hosts. They may also screen calls while the show is on the air. Some producers help the air talent choose topics and generally offer creative assistance when needed.

one medium is the message

Boomers, at least, may recall a time in the '60s, not long after the nation got over bombshelters and "drop drills," when cultural cognoscenti began alerting us to an influence potentially more insidious than any Red Scare: the world domination of the Big Eye. And not just CBS. Pundits were warning of the hazards of watching too much television: grades would fall, social interaction would be disrupted, culture would be debased. Already an entire new world had sprung up around the television, from TV dinners and TV trays to TV Guide. The American home was being dominated by the family television set.

Now at the beginning of the year 2000, it looks as if those predictions are finally coming true. By all accounts, the TV screen will be the nexus for the American home. But not in any way the experts could have foreseen a quarter century ago, back when computers were filled with tubes the size of Big Sticks.

Within a year or two, there will be no media not merged in some way with new media. And the main showcase for that product will be the TV set, which will have as much in common with a Mac monitor as an old Sony. In fact, the time may not be far off when there is only one medium with numerous genres. Like early television, the computer and Internet market has evolved through its first phase of media growth, adopted by a still relatively small but active group of users and consumers. The next stage will see new media become mass media, radically transforming the way we shop, enjoy entertainment, even create and view art. The industry predicts Web advertising revenues to skyrocket from $650 million in 1997 to $8 billion in 2,002.

Making this possible is the widespread adoption of broadband service—sophisticated, high-speed Internet access. This isn't "Omigosh!" futuristic hypothesizing. Two forms of broadband already exist, fighting it out, much like VCR and Betamax in the '80s, in an increasingly down-and-dirty war for the marketplace. One is DSL, digital subscriber lines, which can deliver high-speed, high-capacity access through conventional copper telephone lines; the other is cable modem access, which delivers high-speed, high-capacity digital access through TV cables. The battle has been too close to call, with the nation's corporate forces throwing their money behind one or the other form—or, in the case of AT&T, both. The winner will dominate a market projected to be 20 million broadband users by 2,002.

Whichever wins, the result is the same for the consumer: a revolution in the virtual world. Up until now, the Internet has been a relatively inefficient, low-quality visual and aural experience. Broadband will finally bring once-futuristic three-dimensional images and unthought-of interactive capabilities in e-commerce, the film and television industries, the recording world and the virtual world of Web sites, rendering current Webbies the equivalent of cyber-girdles.

The computer experience will no longer be restricted to simply pouring a traditional medium online. Within the year, users should see the first truly original programming, integrating the real promise of cyberspace: interactivity, the virtual "personal touch." With broadband visuals, advertisers will see those low-tech banner ads attached to Web sites replaced by sophisticated *Star Wars*-like spots, complete with state-of-the-art digital sound, three-dimensional images and technological advances akin to a new generation of CD-ROM.

In addition, consumers for the first time will be able to take part in the ad. While viewing a commercial or video featuring multiple characters, locations and wardrobes, for example, a consumer will be able to click on a given item —a character's Hawaiian shirt, say—and immediately find out the brand, the price and, with another click, order the item to be delivered, all from living room couch. Companies like Veon are already pioneering such technologies to address the so-called "convergence" market. Such advertising opportunities will allow agencies to find partners to share expenses in the transition period from traditional banner advertising to the more sophisticated cyber-advertising that broadband will bring.

Viewing live rock concerts and special events will radically morph. Users will be able to access multiple video feeds at the same time, selecting which group or play or angle they want to see in the "main" window. Foreshadowing the future, Rupert Murdoch's SkyBTV in Britain allows soccer fans to immediately replay a segment from the field or access various angles to replay the action.

Video will surpass all other media as the dominate form online. Every studio now has an Internet division, most notably Sony Picture Entertainment's pioneering CTI division, devoted to promoting and marketing new media potential. In addition, each of the studio's divisions has an interactive unit. Such efforts will transform the television-computer screen into a round-the-clock theater, with viewers able to access films from a limitless library, perhaps any film ever made. More importantly, original content will allow interactive users to click on characters, locations, etc. and navigate into additional video streams or Web sites promoting educational tie-ins, e-commerce, gaming, related titles. Watching an action movie featuring a B-1 bomber, say, a user could simply click on the aircraft and learn the entire history of the development of the plane.

New films online will allow a user to replay certain scenes or, quite possibly, see an alternate version of the scene from another character's point of view. In the ultimate *Rashomon*, the day may come when film directors will shoot several versions of a movie at once, allowing users to, in effect, "create" the story they wish to see.

Other options will enable the user to view a television show or movie on-screen, while at the same time educational or related data while being downloaded to the PC for access after the broadcast is over. While educational opportunities are obvious, entertainment possibilities are limitless. Think of listening to a Top-10 song, a cover of an oldie, for instance, then after the performance, being able to call up music videos by every group that has recorded or performed the tune.

There is much talk by the pundits about the "intersection" of new and old media. But whatever form that takes, convergence or streaming or enhancing, the meeting place will be much more akin to a chemical combustion than a merging, an alchemy that will produce something new, something exciting and something wholly unlooked-for. Here, at the doorstep of tomorrow, Hollywood will have to learn not so much how to navigate the "superhighway" delivering yesterday's goods in a new vehicle, as how to explore the hidden treasures lurking along technology's Yellow Brick Road. ∎

glossary

Above the line: Literally a line on the budget sheet for a film or television show separating "creative talent" (i.e. actors, writers, director, producers) from the rest of the crew (the artisans and craftspeople like the line producer, cinematographer, editor, art director, costumer, etc.) who work hands-on to create the project. Above-the-line talent negotiate their salaries, which usually include some kind of back-end points. The rest of the crew members, known as below the line, usually receive salaries determined by union or guild classifications.

Above-the-title billing: A name credit that precedes the film's title in the opening-credit sequence. Reserved for A-list creatives with the clout to negotiate it in their contracts.

Acquisition: Buying the rights to a project by a distributor from another studio. Most frequently seen when studios buy foreign-film rights from overseas production entities.

ADSL (asymmetric digital subscriber loop): The technology enabling the transmission of digital data via standard copper telephone lines.

Affiliate station: An independent television station which broadcasts a network's daytime and/or prime-time programming in exchange for a fee, advertising time and other prerequisites.

After market: The various revenue markets for distribution of a film or TV project after it has run through its primary release, including TV syndication, home video, cable and Internet downloading.

Air check: A recording or an air talent's on-air performance, leaving out the songs and commercials, called "telescoping" or "scoping."

AKA list: A network or studio's collection of projects in development, which includes both working and alternative titles that can change during the production life of the project.

A-lister: A major actor, writer, director or producer with a proven box-office record who can "guarantee" a film's opening or a TV network executive's attention.

Ambiance: The collection of sounds and music in a film or TV show which normally go unnoticed but nonetheless contribute to the mood of a scene.

Answer print: The first print of a picture complete with the soundtrack.

AQH (Average quarter-hour share): Arbitron's estimate of the average number of persons who have listened to a station for at least five minutes during a 15-minute period.

Arbitron: The Neilsen of radio, the company measures radio audiences in the nation's top 270 markets.

AT: Radio air talent (i.e. DJ, talk-show host, newsperson) with name identification.

ATM (asynchronous transfer mode): High-speed switching technology facilitating the transfer of large volumes of audio-visual data.

Atmospheric: Special effects dealing with wind, water, rain, snow, fog, smoke, fire, etc.

Availability: The times an actor, writer or director is free from existing projects and able to work on a new film or show. Many times used as bargaining leverage to up the salary when two competing studios want the same talent. Also a polite excuse when turning down a project and not wanting to hurt feelings.

Avatar: An online graphical representation of a person using the network which is visible to others online who are accessing or sharing the same virtual environment. Communicating through body movements, text and/or speech, an avatar is an alternative to text-based interactive communication.

Back end: Profit participation paid after a project's release, based on a percentage of the box-office take, as opposed to front-end salary. Reserved for creatives, back end can be anything from net points to gross points and is limited only by the creativity of the talent's attorney.

Back-door pilot: A two-hour TV movie which is not developed as a pilot but is considered to have potential for transformation into an eventual series.

Back list: A studio or network's collection of projects which have not been put into development but which could be put back into the pipeline at any time.

Bandwidth: The amount of data a system is able to carry, measured in hertz (hz).

Beat sheet: A beat-by-beat outline of the major plot points in a story. Also known as "story beats."

Beta test: Software testing by users prior to the formal release of a product or program, designed to uncover problems that may be found in real-world use.

Below the line: The actual costs, including crew salaries, of physically making a movie or television show.

Billing: The position of a cast or crew member's name in the credits, both on-screen and in posters and marketing materials.

Binary code: The base-two numbering system used to record object-code programs.

Blind commitment: Most frequently used in television when a network wants to be associated with a talent, usually a show creator or actor, and promises to commit to an unspecified show in the future. Typically used when a successful show has reached its finale or a promising show has been canceled and the network wants to keep the talent in the stable for the next season.

Boutique agency: A small talent agency with an elite or especially hot clientele.

Breakdowns: Companies that break down scripts in development, detailing parts to be cast and a short description of the role. Sold for a fee to agents and managers.

Broadband: The high-speed delivery platform providing the capability to transmit and receive the largest types of media, such as digitized video content, at the fastest rates possible.

Buy out: When a person, normally a writer or producer, sells out their interest in a project, whether royalties or points, for a lump sum.

Buzz: Word of mouth, a little higher-grade than gossip, buzz is wisdom in the industry about an upcoming film or major business shift—a hiring or firing of a studio head, for example. Industry buzz on an anticipated film, whether good or bad, can directly affect the opening of a movie.

Byte: Typically a group of eight bits, stored and manipulated as a group, generally forming a character of code.

Cable modem: A high-speed modem that receives and delivers data through a coaxial television cable instead of telephone lines.

Caching: A method of storing digital data, such as Web pages, on multiple servers to minimize the time required for material to be downloaded to the end user.

CAD (computer aided design): The digital creation of models, from small tools to buildings, aircraft, and larger objects and environments.

Calling-card film: A film or video which showcases a director or actor's special talents.

Castable: A project that has desirable roles for major talent.

Cast-contingent order: A production order for a project which is subject to the signing of a particular actor, usually an A-lister.

CD-I (compact disc-interactive): An interactive CD-ROM platform developed by Philips and supported by Sony, Matsushita and other hardware manufacturers.

CD-R (compact disc-recordable): A CD-ROM format allowing data to be recorded one time only.

CD-ROM (compact disc-read only memory): A high-density storage media composed of a reflective optical disc, based on the format used for high-fidelity music (CD-DA), the most common data storage formats of CD-ROMs being CD-ROM/XA, CD-I, Photo CD, and CD-R.

CD-V (compact disc-video): An optical-disc format combining analog video with digital stereo.

Character arc: The evolution of the development of a character from the beginning of the script to the end—what the character has learned from the action and how it has changed his or her own actions and sense of self.

Chyron recognition: A celebrity who needs no electronically inserted title or caption (a chyron) to identify him or her on television, especially news programs or interview shows.

Clear-channel station: A class of high-powered (10,000-50,000 watt) nondirectional AM stations operating with protected signals at night, forcing smaller daytime local stations to sign off to avoid interference and clear the airways.

Click-through: Using a computer mouse to click on a Web page advertisement, which takes the user to an intended Web destination.

Client: A computer or program that uses services of another computer or program.

Closed deal: A deal that has been negotiated to everyone's satisfaction and only awaits final signatures by involved parties.

Coder (coder/decoder): A device that converts data from one format to another (such as from analog to digital) for transmission to, or use in, a different kind of delivery system.

Completion bond: An insurance policy required by studios or networks on independent films that guarantees the finances to finish production. If the production company runs out of money, the completion-bond company takes over the film, with the right to replace the producer and the director, in order to ensure the timely and cost-efficient delivery of the film to the studio.

Content: The data that is included, provided or accessible by use of a multimedia application in the form of text, images, audio, film, video or other media.

Coverage: The analysis of a script or teleplay, usually by a reader, including synopsis, potential for casting, marketability, dialogue, action, etc. Producers and agencies use coverage to highlight keepers or weed out scripts that don't show potential.

CPM (cost per thousand): A breakdown of how much it costs advertisers to reach 1,000 listeners on radio.

CPU (central processing unit): The main processing unit of a computer.

Creative executive: Lower-level studio executives who supervise script development for the studio-production executives.

CTR (click-through rate): Calculated by dividing the number of click-throughs by the number of advertising impressions.

Cyberspace: The term coined by science-fiction writer William Gibson to refer to the amorphous environment made up of the World Wide Web and other emerging technologies, referring to time-shifted interaction and access to content.

Dailies: Film footage shot the day before in production, synchronized and projected for producers and studio executives to check on the progress of the film. Also known as "rushes."

Data broadcasting: High-speed data distribution using spare capacity in the broadcast television, cable and satellite transmission systems.

Day part: A specific segment of the radio broadcast day: i.e., "morning-drive time" or "evening."

Deal memo: A short summary of the major deal points between two parties, usually considered binding until the formal contract is signed, though disputed fine points can delay an actual contract for months—and in some cases until the film is already in the can.

Deficit: The difference between the network license fee and the actual cost of producing a TV show. Usually absorbed by the studio and production company until a show goes into syndication.

Development hell: The frustrating and often drawn-out period between the creation, optioning or development of a literary property or concept and the final greenlight to begin shooting. Most projects don't survive this journey.

Digital video: The output of a video camera which has been transformed into a digital format enabling it to be stored and accessed as full-motion video.

Director's cut: The version of a film or TV movie created by the director. Since studios retain the final cut on virtually all movies, this version is not necessarily the movie moviegoers see—unless the distributor, looking to squeeze every last penny out of a project, opts to release the "never before seen" director's cut years later.

Domain names: A unique set of letters, words and/or numbers separated by periods, assigned to each set of media resources made available via the World Wide Web, including a suffix indicating the type of entity that controls the domain, such as .edu (educational), .com (commercial), .org (organizational), .net (networking organization), .mil (military) or .gov (government).

D-person: A lower-level development person who works on the initial acquisition or development of literary properties or concepts for film or television. This group includes readers, story editors and creative affairs vice-presidents—none of whom has the power to say "yes."

DSL (digital subscriber line): A standard twisted-pair telephone line carrying digital signals rather than traditional analog data, increasing the transmission bandwidth.

DSP (digital signal processing): The method of converting and analyzing analog information as digital data.

Duopoly: An ownership arrangement made possible by the relaxation of FCC rules in 1992, which allowed one company to own two AM and two FM stations in the same market. The Telecommunications Act of 1996 created the existence of "superduopolies," in which one company can own up to eight stations in a market.

Edutainment: New media applications and technologies designed both to educate and entertain.

Elements: The key creative talent attached to a project to make it a marketable package to studio executives. Includes cast, writer or writers, director and name producer.

Encryption: The mathematical process of encoding electronic communications in order to protect the information against unauthorized access.

Episodic television: Television series produced in episodes rather than as telefilms or specials.

E&O insurance (errors and omissions insurance): A policy that protects studios and producers from lawsuits arising from copyright infringement, libel or misrepresentation of facts or character. Don't leave home without it.

Executive vice-president of programming: Senior network executive working under the head of programming to determine the content and schedule of prime-time lineups.

Exhibitors: Movie-theater owners who ultimately determine the number of screens and the length of time any given feature will show.

Favored nation: A deal posture by a studio which allows a seller to negotiate a deal on the same terms as a favored producer on the lot. In other words, the person who controls a project is guaranteed the same fees and back end as another producer who has already closed a deal with the studio. Similarly, within the same deal, an actor, for example, could negotiate his or her profit participation structured on the same favored-nation terms as the producer or director.

Fiber-optic cable: A cable with dozens or hundreds of strands of glass and other transparent material known as optic fibers, with each strand carrying light beams modulated to transmit data at capacities exceeding most other means of transmission.

Final cut: The final edited version of a film that is printed and released for distribution. Usually controlled by the studio. (See "director's cut.")

Finger: A program providing information about a user logged on to a given system, such as name, log-in time and terminal location.

Fin/Syn (financial interest and syndication rule): Federal laws which restrict television network ownership and production in the projects they create.

First-look deal: An arrangement by a studio or production company that allows the studio first shot at any project the producer has in development. If the studio passes, the producer can then shop it elsewhere.

Firewall: A combination of hardware and software configured to prevent unauthorized access of a computer network and use of resources connected to the network.

Fish out of water: A proven Hollywood formula in which the hero is thrust into a situation or environment that is totally out of his or her natural element.

Franchise: The Hollywood version of the World Series, the hat trick, the brass ring. A movie or film character that achieves virtual "brand recognition," with bankable characters and presold elements that guarantee multiple sequels and limitless marketing possibilities. Think *Star Wars*, *Star Trek*, *Rocky*, *A Nightmare on Elm Street*. Network executives know going into a project what the bottom-line return will be on any given sequel based on a loyal audience, thus eliminating the risk factor. Even better, franchise properties can be expanded to other mediums, whether through television, the Internet, video or merchandising, giving a studio a guaranteed revenue flow for years, if not decades.

Go picture: A project that has just received a "green light," that is, has been okayed and given a principal production date by a studio.

Golden master: The final version of a product delivered to a commissioning party which has passed approvals and is ready for replication and commercial distribution.

Greenlight: Beulah land. A "yes" by the head of a studio giving the go-ahead for a project in development to be put into production. It is also the time when talent bonuses kick in.

Greenlight power: The handful, literally, of people in the industry who can give the final okay to put a project into production and begin principal photography.

Gross/net revenues or receipts: The measurement of royalties in license agreements, product development, distribution agreements and other commercial multimedia contracts.

Gross points: A back-end deal that stipulates a talent's profit participation is based on a movie's gross take at the box office, as opposed to net take, which is profit after the studio deducts all expenses (what Eddie Murphy described as "monkey points").

GUI (graphical user interface): A style of application user interface utilizing images, icons and graphical material.

Halo effect: The afterglow that shines on the career of everyone who has worked on a hit project. The bigger the hit, the brighter—and longer—the afterglow. Think directors Quentin Tarantino or Sam Mendes.

Handshake deal: A deal in which the two parties agree to the broad points of a contract with a handshake. Far down the deal-making food chain from a deal memo and, usually, not set in stone.

HDTV (high-definition television): The transmission of television signals which produce a higher resolution picture than standard television technology.

Head of programming: Also known as the president of programming or entertainment division president. The main person with TV's version of greenlight authority, responsible for content and scheduling. The buck stops and the ax falls here.

Heat: What all agents, publicists, producers and, ultimately, studio heads want to generate around a project—a great anticipation of success and money.

Hiatus: The downtime in TV production when everyone goes on vacation or does movie projects, usually beginning with the end of production in March and ending in July/August, depending on the show and whether it's a fall premiere or midseason replacement.

High concept: A film or TV story line that lends itself to a one-line pitch—or at least to a 10-minute pitch meeting. These usually involve action pictures or a movie with a gimmick. Hollywood was hot on high-concept in the '80s when producers like Blake Edwards reportedly sold his Bruce Willis-Kim Basinger vehicle *Blind Date* with one line: "Just don't get her drunk." Unfortunately for studio bottom lines, most, like *Blind Date*, sound better than they play.

Hot Java: A browser for creating and viewing World Wide Web documents, allowing the reference of embedded programs, created in Java programming language, to be activated by the user.

Hot maps: A portion of a graphic image that allows a user to connect to another media element.

Housekeeping deal: A deal aimed at keeping a favored producer, director or actor in the studio stable. Usually includes free office space on the back lot, money for development and administrative staff, phone expenses, development money to buy properties and the like. In return, the studio gets not only a degree of loyalty but first look at any projects its star or partner wants to develop. Renowned deals, such as the one offered to Tom Cruise by Paramount in the 1980s, included rental fees on a jet, fuel and personnel costs, along with other nice perks. Some housekeeping deals have been known to include masseuses.

Honey wagon: The most important trailer in the business—the on-location restrooms. Stars, of course, have their own personal trailers.

Host: The main computer in a system of computers or terminals.

Hot seat: Literally, the operating seat of a camera-crane operator; more generally, any producer or studio executive with a project in production—especially one behind schedule and over budget.

HTML (hypertext markup language): The programming language used to format documents for viewing through a browser on a computer, typically on a network or the Internet, which allows the browser to display textual type, images and other multimedia, and permits interaction through elements embedded within the document.

HTTP (hypertext transfer protocol): The standard for communication between browser software and servers on the World Wide Web, defining how documents are referenced and exchanged.

Hyphenate: A double, sometimes triple-threat talent, as in writer-director, or, like Quentin Tarantino, writer-director-actor. More common in TV, where most creators are also writer/executive producers.

Impression: The number of times an advertisement is displayed and viewed.

Infotainment: The new media applications and technology created to both inform and entertain.

Indie production: An independent production company which finds, develops and finances its own films, then negotiates a distribution deal with a major studio. In recent years, the most renowned companies, like Miramax (which merged with Disney) have been purchased by big studios. Still, indies like New Line and upstart Artisan, which boasted the summer '99 surprise blockbuster *The Blair Witch Project* continue to offer an alternative to Hollywood's Big Seven.

Institutional market: Hollywood's version of the trade publication: films aimed at providing information to a defined group such as schools, medical facilities, airlines, the armed forces and even prisons.

Interactive: The term generally used to refer to the ability of hardware and software to respond to input from users in a non-linear fashion, allowing a user to control the presentation.

Interaction rate: The percentage of online users that interact with an advertisement. Divided by the number of impressions served.

Interactive television: Video programming content designed to allow the viewer to communicate with the content provider.

IP (Internet protocol): The technical specification that determines the transmission of data across the Internet.

Interstitial: Typically an advertisement which is seen between Web pages or other content and is usually smaller than a full page. Usually an interstitial must be viewed in it entirety, or the viewer must make an effort to remove it from the screen.

IRC (Internet relay chat): A real-time chat service based on a client-server system (modeled on CB radio) ordering discussions into hundreds of channels, with every user having an unique identity.

Java: A programming language providing sound, interactive features, moving graphics and access to remote data files and other features.

JPEG (joint photographic experts group): A compression standard for compressing still photographic images in digital format.

JSA: A joint sales agreement in which two radio stations sell advertisers their combined markets for the price of one buy, usually national.

KBPS: Thousands (kilos) of bits per second. Measurement of the speed at which data is transferred.

Kilobyte: Referring to 1,024 bytes, also abbreviated as "K."

Kiosk: A freestanding PC providing information to the public, usually through a multimedia display, with data often provided through the Internet.

LAN (local area network): Primarily a private computer network covering a small area, such as a single building or office area.

Legs: A movie that not only opens well but continues to play well at the box office weeks or months after the first crucial week.

License fee: The money paid by a network to a production company or studio to obtain the programming rights to a TV series, giving the network a guaranteed number of exclusive broadcasts (usually an original and one or two repeats) in a specified time (usually four years).

LMA (local marketing agreement): An agreement between two local radio stations in which one markets and sells advertising for the other for either a fee or a percentage of profits.

Log line: A one-sentence description of a literary product—book, play, screenplay, etc.

Looping: The recording of an actor's voice in the studio after the scene has already been shot.

Megabyte: One million bytes of data.

Meta data: Data which describes other data, typically imbedded within a media file such as an HTML document, describing such information as a title, subject, author and size of a file.

MIDI (musical instrument digital interface): An industry standard for producing, recording and embodying digital audio signals in multimedia applications and communicating digital audio between input and output devices.

MOS: A scene shot without sound, from German director Eric von Stroheim's immortal command: "Mitt out sound!"

Most favored nation: See "Favored nation."

Movie cross: Development shorthand to describe the concept of a project using known movies—e.g., "It's kind of a *Star Wars* meets *High Noon*, or a *Blair Witch Project* meets *The Exorcist*." "Yeah? Let's take a meeting."

Movie jail: The other end of "heat," or where a director or actor lands after one or two box-office bombs. Most recently, Richard Gere and John Travolta both waited years to post bond after a succession of near-fatal duds like *King David* and *Perfect*, respectively.

MPAA (The Motion Picture Association of America): The industry trade group which not only oversees the all-important movie-ratings system but also represents industry lobbying efforts in Washington under longtime head Jack Valenti.

MPEG (motion picture experts group): The standard for digital compression and decompression of video and audio content, often part of the technical requirements specified in development agreements.

Multimedia: Applications or environments involving the interactive use of text, audio, images, film, video, photography and graphics.

Negative pickup: A deal where a studio guarantees a set fee to release a movie produced by an independent producer, based on the cost of shooting the film and creating a negative. The independent producer uses the distribution deal to raise financing from various sources in order to produce the film.

Net profits: The profits of a film after all studio and production expenses have been deducted. This basically means box-office share minus talent fees (front end and back end), production costs, equipment rental, insurance costs, studio overhead, interest, distribution and marketing and anything else remotely connected to the creation of the film.

Network approved: A list of writers, show runners, directors and actors deemed acceptable and employable by a network. Nobodies need not apply.

Network share: The percentage of the television viewing audience turned into a network on any given night of programming.

Nursery man: The individual who supplies plants to a movie set or location shot. Not to be confused with the baby wrangler.

Off network: A television series that has completed its network licensing run and is eligible for syndication.

One sheet: A movie poster, the kind mounted in theater marquees.

One-sheet lines: The one-line grabber or phrase that heads the one sheet and forms the marketing theme. *Alien*'s classic: "In space, no one can hear you scream."

O&O: Abbreviation that denotes a television station that is "owned and operated by" a particular company.

Online: The data communications capability of a computer linked to other computers.

Open: How a movie performs at the box office in the first five days of its release.

Opener: An actor, more rarely a director (à la Woody Allen), whose celebrity and track record can be counted on to draw a loyal following and guarantee at least a respectable opening.

Option: A deal in which a sum is paid to secure the exclusive rights to a literary property for a specified time period, usually six months to a year. The option includes a provision to buy the property at expiration. During that time, the producer will try to develop the project at a studio, laying off the option or purchase price on the studio.

Orphan: A project that finds itself suddenly without backing when its champion at the studio or production company leaves or loses favor in a management change.

P&A (prints and advertising): The studio cost of printing negatives of a film for distribution to theaters and all marketing and advertising costs, including print, television, radio and special promotions. This can run as high as a quarter of a film's entire production budget.

Packaging: The practice of talent agencies to bundle together the major elements of a film project—writer, director, actor, even producer—then sell the entire package ready-made to a studio. Agencies then commission 10 percent of the entire package rather than charging a separate commission on each client. The package was a seductive quick fix in the 1980s to studio heads feeling pressure from huge corporate owners and looking for some kind of big-name box office guarantee. The package, however, produced some of the decade's most infamous bombs and fell out of favor in the more cost-conscious late '90s.

Pay or play: A deal in which a studio or production company is obligated to pay a talent's entire salary whether or not he or she is actually used in the project. Actors, directors and, especially, writers see pay or play as a necessity in an industry notorious for employing "replacement parts."

PCM (pulse code modulation): The process of converting analog signals to digital equivalents.

Phone monkey: Executives who spend the day schmoozing and deal making on their cellular phones.

PIC (picture image compression): A standard for compressing still images.

Pitch: A short verbal presentation of a film idea to a producer or studio executive designed not only to convey the plot and characters but make them want to buy the project. If successful, the next step is a development deal to create an acceptable script.

Pixel (picture element): Extremely small locations on a screen which are combined to produce screen images, with higher resolution images having a larger pixel count.

Plug and play: The capability of a hardware device to plug into PCs without any manual configuration of the system, and the ability of software to work with other software components without any special configuration.

Polish: A minor rewrite of a script, perhaps tightening the dialogue, working up some jokes or reworking the weaker scenes.

Postproduction: The final phase of production following principal photography, including sound mixing and remixing, foley work, editing and rough cuts.

PGP (pretty good privacy): An implementation of RSA encryption technology made available on a commercial basis.

Platform: The hardware, operating system and device format on which a particular application executes.

PLV (production-level video compression): The highest level of compression creating VCR-quality images.

Principal photography: The actual filming of the movie on the set or location.

Product: General term for any film or television show.

Production bonus: A guaranteed contractual payment made to a writer upon the commencement of principal photography.

Production order: The official commissioning of a show by a television network.

Production values: The quality of the final visual and audio result seen on the screen. Also, the amount of money per minute of screening time it cost to attain those results.

Profit participation: The same thing as back end, the sharing of a film's profits subject to a contractual definition of net or gross points and what "profit" is to be participated in: first dollar gross, rolling gross, etc.

Property: The literary material that forms the basis of a film or TV show: book, play, magazine article, screenplay, treatment, etc.

Protocol: Rule or agreement covering network communications features.

Public key/private key: The encryption of data using code corresponding to a unique decryption code held by the recipient called the private key, with a single private key generating any number of compatible public keys.

Quote: The salary a talent was paid for his or her last project. It forms the starting point of negotiations on the new deal.

RAM (random access memory): Memory residing in the computer from which applications function.

Repurpose: The adaptation of preexisting works as content.

Residuals: Payments made to talent upon rebroadcasting of a television show or movie. Based on a percentage of the original salary, residuals can go on for decades (think *The Brady Bunch*) and, depending on how many foreign markets carry syndications, can be substantial.

Reversions: License provisions limiting the risk on the part of the licensor by causing rights to revert back to the licensor if the commercialization of the product by the licensee has not reached certain economic expectations within a specified time frame.

Rights holder: The person who controls the rights to a property.

Rolling gross: A definition used in determining profit participation. It is an agreed-upon formula that allows the studio to deduct defined expenses before profit is reached, including the negative cost of the film (what it cost to make it), studio overhead, insurance, and all talent back end. It is similar to adjusted gross—and a long way from first-dollar gross, in which a talent's participation kicks in with the first ticket sold at the box office.

Rough cut: The editor's first complete version of a film, including sound.

RSA: A public-key encryption system for private use, taking advantage of the difficulty in factoring very large numbers that are the product of two prime numbers, enabling each user to lock his/her encrypted information with a a unique public key for that user.

SAG (The Screen Actors Guild): The union which represents actors in collective bargaining, setting the basic working contracts of actors and handling health and other benefits.

Scalable: Content created to maximize the viewing experience for the capabilities of a variety of viewers.

Sell-through: Home video tapes of a film which are sold to retail customers.

Server: A computer controlling access to a network and resources such as a printer and file sharing, including the machines which deliver media through the Internet.

Share: The percentage of radio listeners in a market tuned to a given station.

Shopping: Pitching a property which one does not have the rights to, hoping to interest a studio first, and then finding the funding to purchase the rights.

Short list: The pared-down casting list of talent a studio or producer wants to use on a project.

Show-runner: A writer-producer who is in charge of producing a television show and getting it to the network on schedule.

Source code escrow: Retention of a neutral third party to hold the source code and other trade secrets and proprietary information related to the development of software, serving to provide security for the licensee against the failure of the licensor's development work.

Spec script: A screenplay written on speculation to be sold to a studio or producer, as opposed to a commissioned screenplay.

Step outline: An outline of a all three acts in a screenplay, with one sentence describing each scene.

Step-up: Contractual clauses that call for bump-ups in payments in the event of special circumstances; i.e., a TV movie project is bumped up to a feature film.

Streaming: The process of delivering video and audio content online in real time, not requiring a complete file download before viewing, using software such as RealVideo or NetShow.

Stunt casting: Attaching names to a project in development to make it a more desirable package.

Submission: Written material sent to a studio or producer by an agent, executive or writer.

Suit: A studio executive.

Syndication: Refers to first-run syndication or the release of a show that has completed its licensing agreement and is independently sold for rebroadcast. Such a show is referred to as "in syndication."

Telephone pass: The rejection of a submission by an executive or producer over the phone—the usual way of saying "no" in Hollywood.

Teleplay: A script written for a TV movie, as opposed to a screenplay.

Tent pole: The supposedly can't-miss projects on a studio's film slate that will create the financial umbrella to protect the smaller movies.

Tiered royalties: License-provision arrangement allocating risk between licensor and licensee by limiting royalty payments to the licensor until the product revenues cover production costs, usually allowing for increased royalty payments as the product reaches specific revenue milestones.

Topper: Trade mag-ese for the head of a studio, such as Disney topper Michael Eisner.

The Town: Hollywood—the industry, not the city.

Time to market: The time it takes for a program to go from initial concept to product shipment to the market.

Trailer: A short montage of film footage from an upcoming movie used to build buzz among audiences.

Transfer rate: The amount of information that can be moved from a compact disc to RAM per second.

Treatment: A short description of a movie, including major story beats, characters and setting, usually five to ten pages.

TSL (time spent listening): Arbitron's estimate of the number of quarter hours the average radio listener spends with a specific station during a specified time period.

Turnaround: Usually the first stages of development hell. A studio that has decided not to go forward with a project can put it in turnaround, which means another studio can acquire the project by paying back development costs to date. Rare is the project that makes the turn.

Underlying rights: The rights to the material which are the basis for a screenplay.

Unsolicited submission: A screenplay sent unbidden to a studio by an unknown writer without an agent. Usually returned unread.